enrich-e-matics
3rd EDITION

BOOK 1

Anne Joshua

MA, Dip Ed (Syd); MSc (Oxon)

enrich-e-matics
3rd EDITION

Dear Teachers, Students and Parents,

Thank you for purchasing *Enrich-e-matics 3rd Edition*. This is the first of a series of six books designed to develop and enrich students' problem-solving skills. *Enrich-e-matics 3rd Edition* deepens students' mathematical concepts and encourages flexibility of thinking along with a willingness to tackle challenging and fascinating problems. The series was originally designed to cater for the mathematically able student but was also found to be a useful tool for all schools wishing to strengthen their students' mathematical understanding.

What is different about *Enrich-e-matics 3rd Edition*?

Enrich-e-matics 3rd Edition is much more than a collection of puzzles and difficult problems. The exercises are *graded*. Concepts and strategies are developed throughout the series to provide for a systematic development of problem-solving and mathematical ability.

The exercises and activities have been grouped into mathematics strands—**Number, Patterns & Algebra, Chance & Data, Measurement, Space** and **Working Mathematically**—with hundreds of new problems added. This allows students and teachers to work systematically through a number of similar problems focusing on one area of mathematics. It also allows flexibility of programming so that material from different strands can be integrated. The strand is indicated on each page by an icon. Themes are introduced and developed throughout the series. The answers for all problems are included in a removable section at the back of the book.

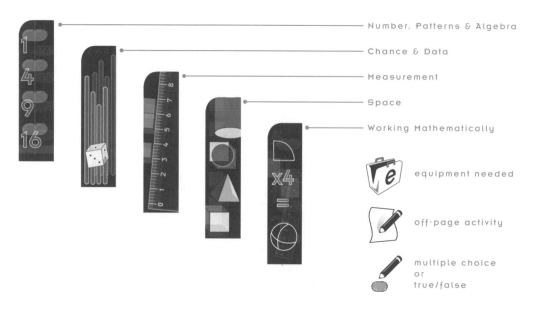

In *Enrich-e-matics 3rd Edition* explanations and worked examples are highlighted. The space for students to write answers and show their working has been maximised in this new edition. An icon has been used to show where students may need extra paper or equipment to complete the problems. Multiple choice and true/false questions use shaded bubbles similar to those used in state and national test papers. ⬭

Enrich-e-matics 3rd Edition is designed to meet the needs of students by:

- providing challenging problems for enrichment and extension
- reinforcing concepts and skills
- developing problem-solving strategies and extending mathematical insight, ability and logical thought
- providing opportunities to experience the joy of problem solving
- providing a ready source of challenging problems to prepare students for mathematics competitions

all of which build the foundation for excellence in mathematics.

The *Enrich-e-matics* series may be used to supplement and be integrated into the school's mathematics program.

The *Enrich-e-matics 3rd Edition Teacher's Book* is available to assist teachers implement the enrichment program in their school. It is a most valuable resource containing teaching suggestions, worked solutions and reproducible material. Most importantly it also contains highly valued screening tests that help to identify mathematical ability.

Who can use this book?

Enrich-e-matics 3rd Edition Book 1 may be used by:

- a group of able students working together in class
- classes in selective schools or maths extension groups
- an individual student at home.

The books have been extensively trialled, over several years, with students aged 6 to 15 in schools and at various camps for gifted and talented students. *Enrich-e-matics 3rd Edition Book 1* is aimed at 6 to 8 year olds.

To gain the maximum advantage from the series encourage students to discuss their solutions in small groups, with their teacher or with parents at home. This discussion of ideas enhances learning.

I hope that you will find *Enrich-e-matics 3rd Edition* enjoyable and challenging, and that you remain curious and motivated mathematics students.

Anne Joshua

Contents

ANSWERS
lift-out at the back of book

Total of ten

Fill in the blank cards to make a total of 10.

1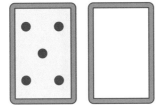

2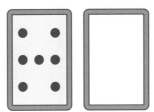

3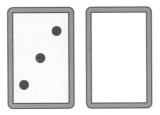

4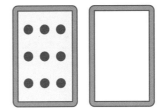

5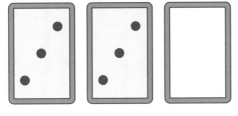

6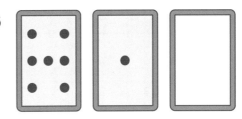

7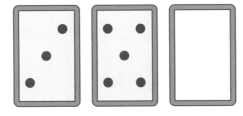

8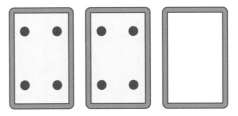

9

10

Total of twelve

Fill in the blank cards to make a total of 12.

1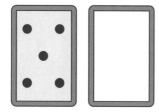

2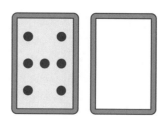

3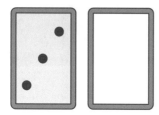

4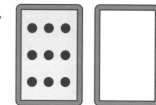

5

6

7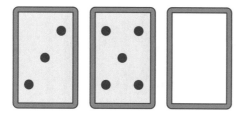

8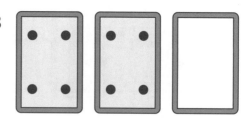

9

10

Number sentences

 Equipment: 10 counters

Use 1, 2, 3, 4 or 5 in each question to complete the number sentences.

Work out your answers by trying different counters in the spaces.

1   2 + _____ = 3   **2**   3 + _____ = 5

3   1 + _____ = 6   **4**   4 + _____ = 8

5   2 + _____ = 7   **6**   6 + _____ = 7

7   6 + _____ = 10   **8**   4 – _____ = 1

9   6 – _____ = 2   **10**   8 – _____ = 3

11   6 – _____ = 4   **12**   5 – _____ = 2

13   7 – _____ = 3   **14**   _____ – 3 = 2

Add or subtract

To make 5 ☐ 3 = 8 into a number sentence,
we need the symbol +, since 5 + 3 = 8.

To make 5 ☐ 3 = 2 into a number sentence,
we need the symbol −, since 5 − 3 = 2.

In the following questions, write the missing + or − signs in the boxes to make a number sentence.

1 3 ☐ 2 = 5

2 2 ☐ 1 = 1

3 4 ☐ 2 = 2

4 4 ☐ 5 = 9

5 7 ☐ 4 = 3

6 7 ☐ 3 = 10

7 4 ☐ 4 = 0

8 10 ☐ 9 = 1

9 4 ☐ 2 = 6

10 4 ☐ 3 = 1

11 8 ☐ 2 = 6

12 8 ☐ 2 = 10

13 6 ☐ 2 = 8

14 9 ☐ 2 = 7

15 10 ☐ 10 = 20

16 10 ☐ 3 = 7

Number patterns

To find the next two numbers in the pattern 2, 5, 8, 11, _____ , _____ we need to look at the differences between the numbers.

Write down the next two numbers in these patterns.

1   5,   7,   9,   11,   _____ , _____

2   1,   4,   7,   10,   _____ , _____

3   15,   13,   11,   9,   _____ , _____

4   4,   6,   8,   10,   _____ , _____

5   5,   10,   15,   20,   _____ , _____

6   10,   20,   30,   40,   _____ , _____

7   90,   80,   70,   60,   _____ , _____

8   3,   13,   23,   33,   _____ , _____

9   11,   22,   33,   44,   _____ , _____

10   24,   22,   20,   18,   _____ , _____

What comes next?

Write down the next two numbers in these patterns.

1 12, 15, 18, 21, _____ , _____

2 3, 6, 9, 12, _____ , _____

3 18, 17, 16, 15, _____ , _____

4 88, 77, 66, 55, _____ , _____

5 21, 19, 17, 15, _____ , _____

6 35, 30, 25, 20, _____ , _____

7 11, 21, 31, 41, _____ , _____

8 4, 14, 24, 34, _____ , _____

9 23, 20, 17, 14, _____ , _____

10 22, 24, 26, 28, _____ , _____

11 40, 35, 30, 25, _____ , _____

12 30, 28, 26, 24, _____ , _____

13 87, 77, 67, 57, _____ , _____

14 1, 5, 9, 13, _____ , _____

Continue the pattern

Look for a pattern in the numbers below and continue it for the rest of the line. It might help you to read the pattern aloud.

1   8642 8642 8642   ____ ____ ____

2   12345 12345 12345   _____ _____

3   357 99 357 99   ___ __ ___ __

4   1223 1223 1223   ____ ____ ____

5   9876 9876 9876   ____ ____ ____

6   2468 2468 2468   ____ ____ ____

7   220 30 220 30 220   __ ___ __ ___

8   7339 7339 7339   ____ ____ ____

9   5445 5445 5445   ____ ____ ____

10   97579 97579 97579   _____ _____

11   5311 5311 5311   ____ ___ ____

12   123 321 123 321   ___ ___ ___ ___

Bricks

A tower of bricks is built so that each new brick that is placed on top of two bricks is the sum of the numbers on these two bricks.

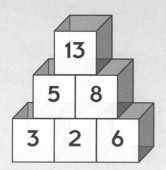

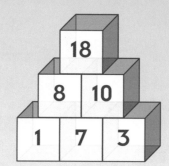

Find the value of each missing brick.

1

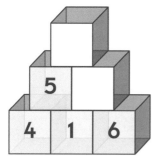

2

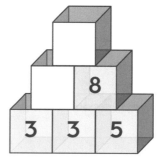

3

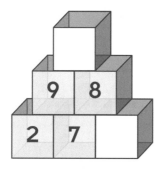

4

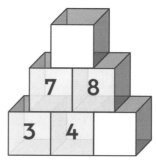

5

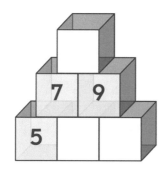

6

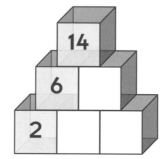

Counter puzzles

 Equipment: one set of counters numbered 1, 2, 3, 4, 5 and 6

Place counters in the circles to help work out these puzzles.

1   Place the numbers 3, 4
and 5 in the circles so that
the sum of the numbers in
each line is 8.

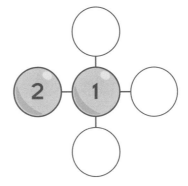

2   Place the numbers 1, 4
and 5 in the circles so that
the sum of the numbers in
each line is 9.

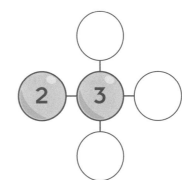

3   Place the numbers 1, 2
and 3 in the circles so that
the sum of the numbers in
each line is 10.

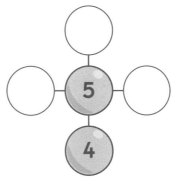

4   Place the numbers 3, 5
and 6 in the circles so that
the sum of the numbers in
each line is 12.

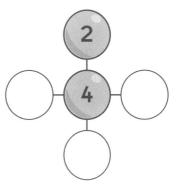

What number fits?

Equipment: one set of counters numbered 1, 2, 3, 4, 5, 6 and 7

Place counters in the circles to help work out these puzzles.

1 Place the numbers 4, 5 and 6 in the circles so that the sum of the numbers in each line is 15.

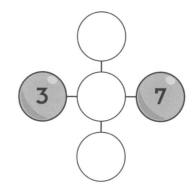

2 Place the numbers 3, 4 and 6 in the circles so that the sum of the numbers in each line is 16.

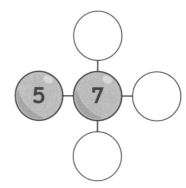

3 Arrange the numbers 3, 4, 5, 6 and 7 in the circles so that the sum of the numbers in each line is 10.

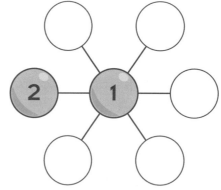

4 Arrange the numbers 2, 3, 4, 5 and 6 in the circles so that the sum of the numbers in each line is 14.

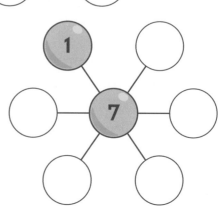

Number, Patterns & Algebra

10

Place the numbers

Equipment: one set of counters numbered 1, 2, 3, 4 and 5

1   Place the numbers 2, 3, 4 and 5 in the circles so that the sum of the numbers in each line is 8.

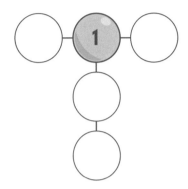

2   Place the numbers 1, 2, 4 and 5 in the circles so that the sum of the numbers in each line is 9.

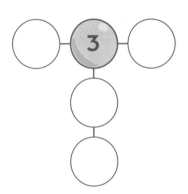

3   Place the numbers 1, 2, 3 and 4 in the circles so that the sum of the numbers in each line is 10.

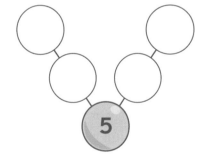

4   Place the numbers 1, 2, 3 and 4 in the circles so that the sum of the numbers in each line is 7.

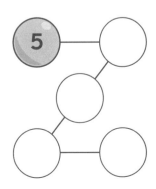

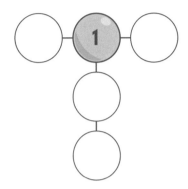

Numbers in circles

Equipment: one set of counters numbered 1, 2, 3, 4, 5 and 6

Place counters in the circles to work out these puzzles.

You may have to guess and then check your guess a few times to find the correct solution.

The numbers 1, 2, 3 and 4 are arranged in the two circles so that each circle has two numbers in it and the sum of these two numbers in each circle is the same.

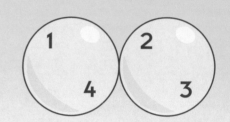

1 Place the numbers 1, 2 and 3 in the three circles, so that each circle has two numbers in it and the sum of these two numbers in each circle is the same.

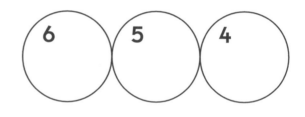

2 Arrange the numbers 1, 2 and 5 in the circles, so that the sum of the numbers in each line is 10.

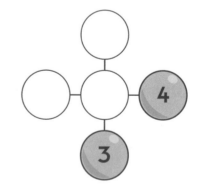

3 Arrange the numbers 1, 2, 3 and 4 in the circles so that the sum of the numbers in each line is 12.

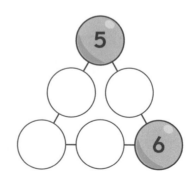

Number, Patterns & Algebra

12

Numbers in triangles

Equipment: one set of counters numbered 1, 2, 3, 4, 5 and 6

1   Place the numbers 2, 3, 4 and 5 in the circles so that the sum of the numbers in each line is 9.

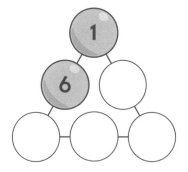

2   Place the numbers 4, 5 and 6 in the circles so that the sum of the numbers in each line is 12.

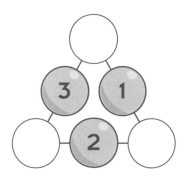

3   Place the numbers 1, 3 and 4 in the circles so that the sum of the numbers in each line is 9.

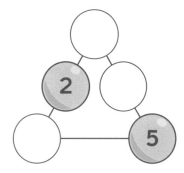

4   Place the numbers 3, 4, 5 and 6 in the circles so that the sum of the numbers in each line is 10.

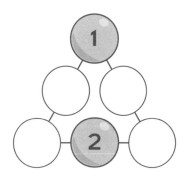

Abacus numbers

Write down the number shown on the abacus.

The first one has been done for you.

1

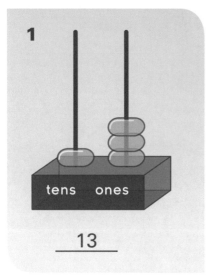

tens ones

13

2

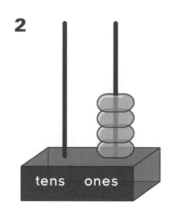

tens ones

_____

3

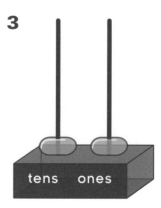

tens ones

_____

4

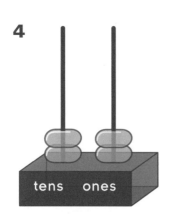

tens ones

_____

5

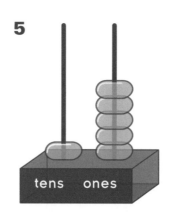

tens ones

_____

6

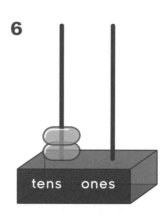

tens ones

_____

7

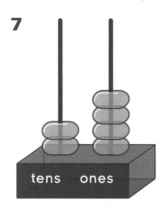

tens ones

_____

8

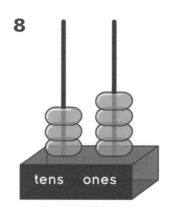

tens ones

_____

9

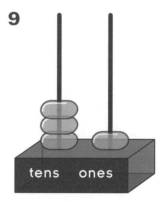

tens ones

_____

Which abacus number?

Write down the number shown on the abacus.

The first one has been done for you.

1

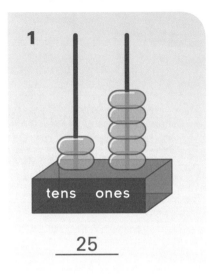

tens   ones

25

2

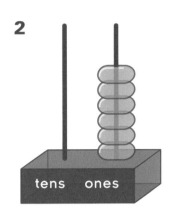

tens   ones

———

3

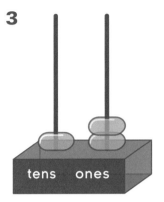

tens   ones

———

4

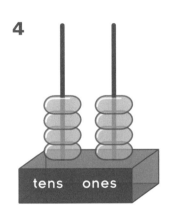

tens   ones

———

5

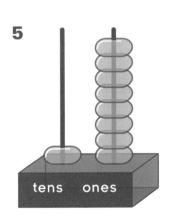

tens   ones

———

6

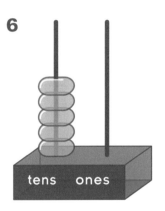

tens   ones

———

7

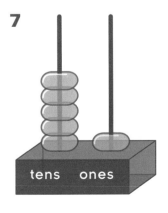

tens   ones

———

8

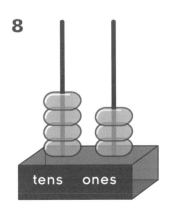

tens   ones

———

9

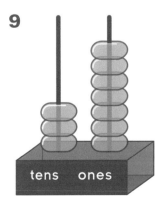

tens   ones

———

Abacus addition

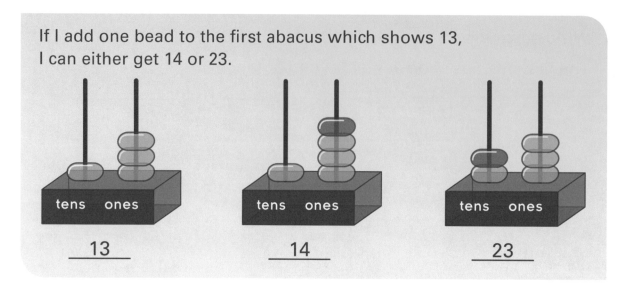

If I add one bead to the first abacus which shows 13,
I can either get 14 or 23.

_____13_____   _____14_____   _____23_____

Above each abacus, write the number shown on the abacus. Then
below each abacus, write what number will be shown on the
abacus, if one bead is added to the 'tens' or the 'ones'.

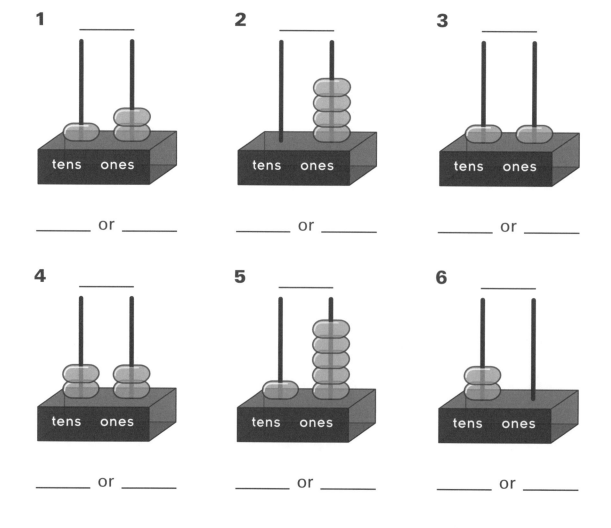

1 _____

_____ or _____

2 _____

_____ or _____

3 _____

_____ or _____

4 _____

_____ or _____

5 _____

_____ or _____

6 _____

_____ or _____

Abacus subtraction

If I take one bead from the first abacus which shows 13,
I can either get 3 or 12.

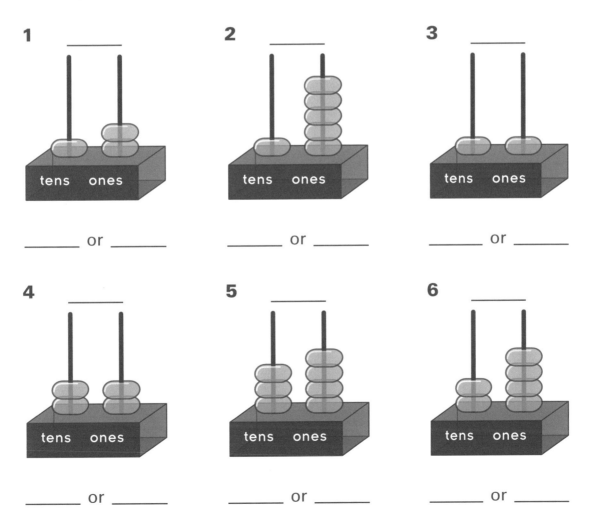

tens ones   tens ones   tens ones

_13_   _3_   _12_

Above each abacus, write the number shown on the abacus. Then
below each abacus, write what number will be shown on the
abacus, if one bead is taken from the 'tens' or the 'ones'.

1 _____

tens ones

_____ or _____

2 _____

tens ones

_____ or _____

3 _____

tens ones

_____ or _____

4 _____

tens ones

_____ or _____

5 _____

tens ones

_____ or _____

6 _____

tens ones

_____ or _____

Abacus challenge

If you have five beads, you can write the number 23 or 14 on the abacus as shown below.

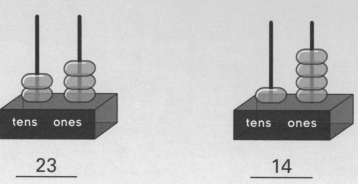

23   14

1 Using these five beads, what other numbers can you make on the abacus? Draw the beads and write the number under each picture.

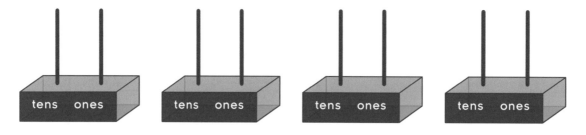

_____   _____   _____   _____

2 What numbers can you make on the abacus if you have three beads?

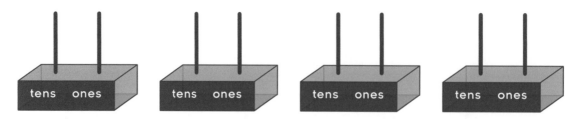

_____   _____   _____   _____

3 **a** What is the largest number you can make using six beads? _____

b What is the smallest number you can make using six beads? _____

Number, Patterns & Algebra

Grid sums

In these grids, the sum of the numbers in each row and the sum of the numbers in each column is given. For example:

- in question 1: 3 + 1 = 4 and 1 + 3 = 4
- in question 2: 3 + 2 = 5 and 2 + 5 = 7

Find the missing numbers in each grid.

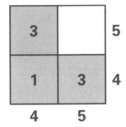

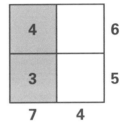

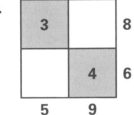

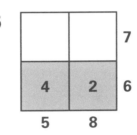

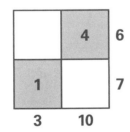

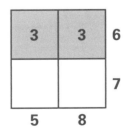

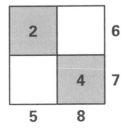

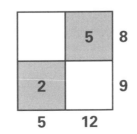

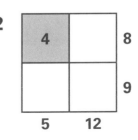

Find my start

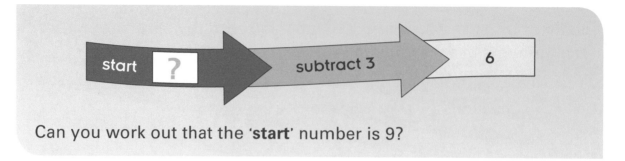

start [?] → subtract 3 → 6

Can you work out that the 'start' number is 9?

What is the number in the **start** box in each case?
Write it in the white box.

1

start [ ] → add 2 → 10

2

start [ ] → subtract 4 → 8

3

start [ ] → add 5 → 13

4

start [ ] → subtract 5 → 7

5

start [ ] → subtract 9 → 13

6

start [ ] → double → 12

7

start [ ] → double → add 1 → 9

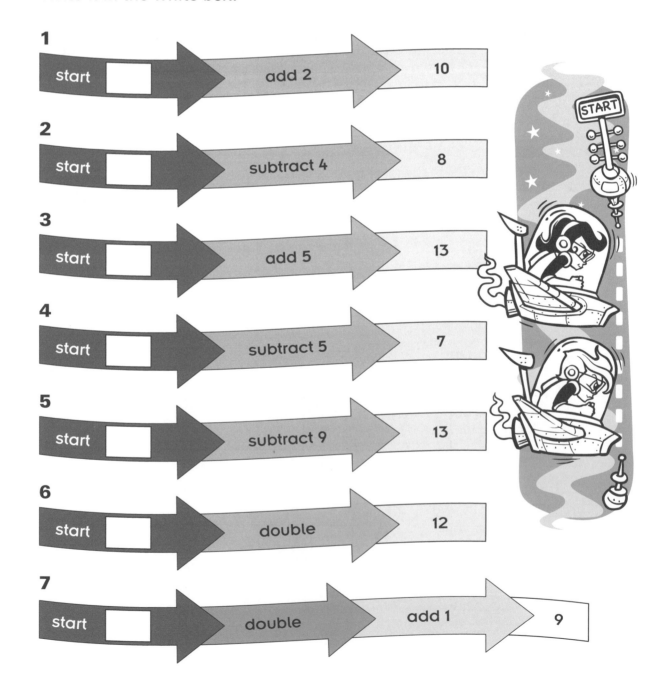

Parts of shapes

What part of each shape is coloured? Check the first three examples carefully.

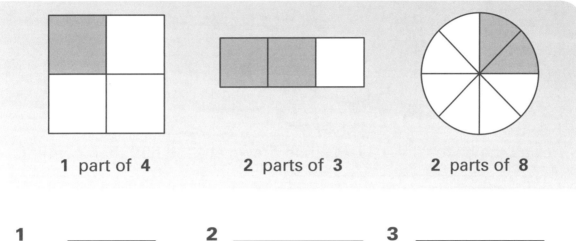

1 part of **4**   **2** parts of **3**   **2** parts of **8**

1

_____ parts of _____

2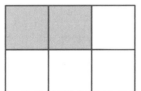

_____ parts of _____

3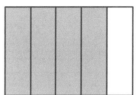

_____ parts of _____

4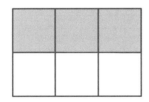

_____ parts of _____

5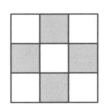

_____ parts of _____

6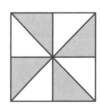

_____ parts of _____

7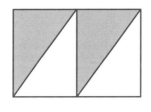

_____ parts of _____

8

_____ parts of _____

9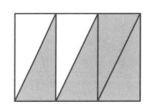

_____ parts of _____

Number, Patterns & Algebra

Fractions

In this box one half of all the planets have a circle drawn around them.

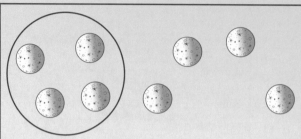

Tick all the boxes that have a circle drawn around half their contents.

1
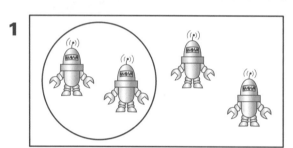

2
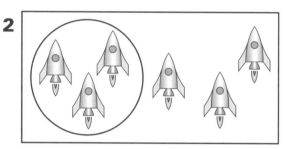

3
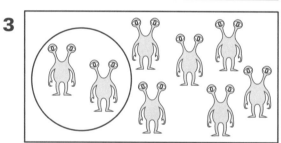

4
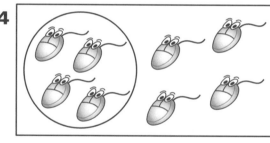

5
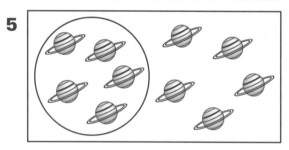

6
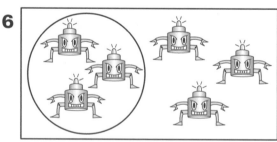

7
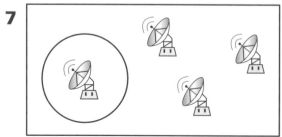

8
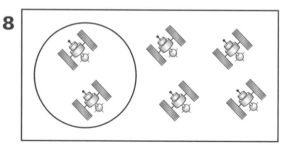

Colour in those circles that hold **one quarter** of all the objects in the box.

Find the value

If the value of the shaded part is 4c,
then the value of the whole shape is 16c.

c = cents

The value of the shaded part of each shape below is given.
What is the value of the whole shape?

1

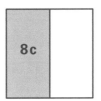

8c

_____

2

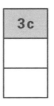

3c

_____

3

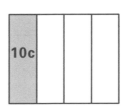

10c

_____

4

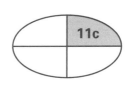

11c

_____

5

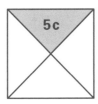

5c

_____

6

2c

_____

7

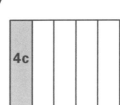

4c

_____

8

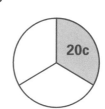

20c

_____

9

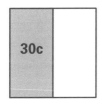

30c

_____

10

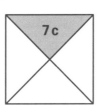

7c

_____

11

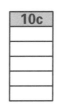

10c

_____

12

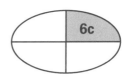

6c

_____

Halves and quarters

Draw pictures in the empty boxes to work out these problems.

Find how many apples I have, if:

1 half of all the
apples I have is 2. _____

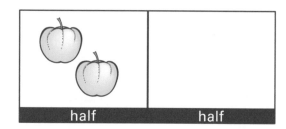

2 half of all the
apples I have is 5. _____

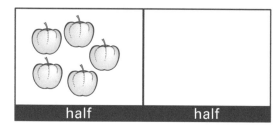

3 half of all the
apples I have is 7. _____

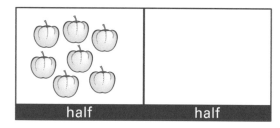

4 one quarter of all
the apples I have is 2. _____

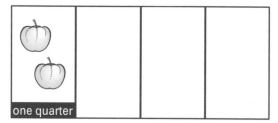

5 one quarter of all
the apples I have is 3. _____

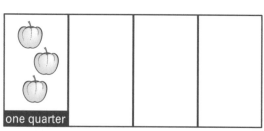

6 one quarter of all
the apples I have is 5. _____

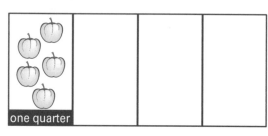

Number, Patterns & Algebra

How many apples?

Complete the pictures to help you work out these problems.

Find how many apples I have, if:

1 $\frac{1}{2}$ of all the apples I have is 4.

I have _____
apples altogether.

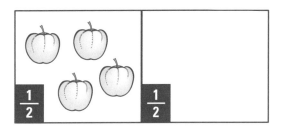

2 $\frac{1}{2}$ of all the apples I have is 10.

I have _____
apples altogether.

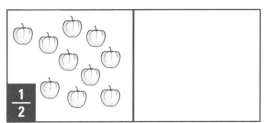

3 $\frac{1}{3}$ of all the apples I have is 2.

I have _____
apples altogether.

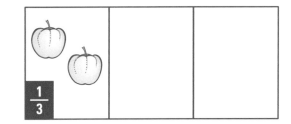

4 $\frac{1}{4}$ of all the apples I have is 2.

I have _____
apples altogether.

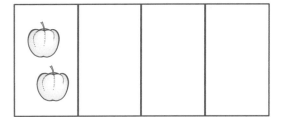

5 $\frac{1}{3}$ of all the apples I have is 5.

I have _____
apples altogether.

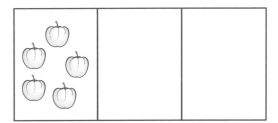

6 $\frac{1}{4}$ of all the apples I have is 6.

I have _____
apples altogether.

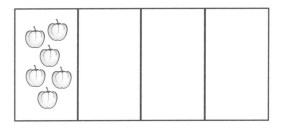

Number line

On this number line, the markings are equally spaced.

We can try to count in ones but this does not work.
When we count in twos along the markings we get to 8, so ☆ = 4.

If the markings on the number line are equally spaced, what is the number ☆ in each question? Write the answer in the star.
In some questions you may have to count in 3s or 5s.

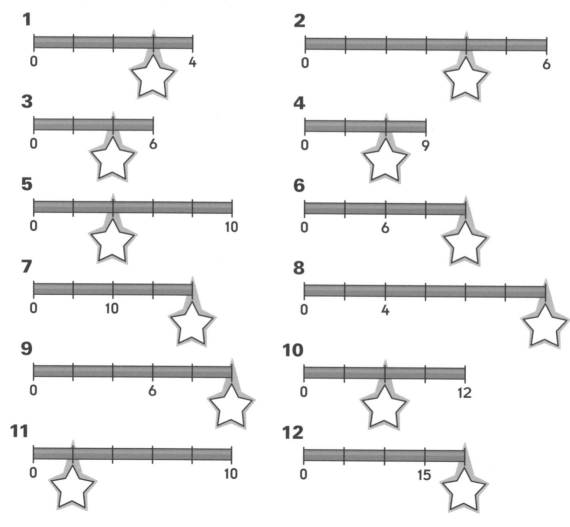

Bowling pins

Lane 1

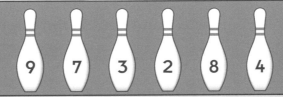

9 7 3 2 8 4

If Lauren knocked down two bowling pins and she scored 5 points, we can work out that she knocked down a 3 and a 2 bowling pin.

1 Which two bowling pins did she knock down if she scored:

a 9? _____ and _____

b 12? _____ and _____

2 Which three bowling pins did she knock down if she scored:

a 12? _____ and _____ and _____

b 14? _____ and _____ and _____

Lane 2

6 3 8 5 7 4 9

3 Which two pins did she knock down in lane 2 if she scored:

a 11? _____ and _____

b 13? _____ and _____

4 Which three pins did she knock down in lane 2 if she scored:

a 15? _____ and _____ and _____

b 17? _____ and _____ and _____

5 Which four pins did she knock down in lane 2 if she scored 20?

_____ and _____ and _____ and _____

Missing numbers

1 The number in the circle is the sum of the numbers in the square and the triangle. Find the missing numbers.

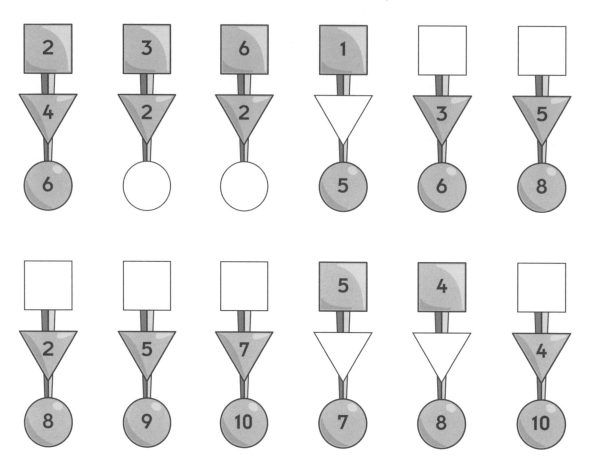

2 If you take away the number in the triangle from the number in the square, you will get the number in the circle. Find the missing numbers.

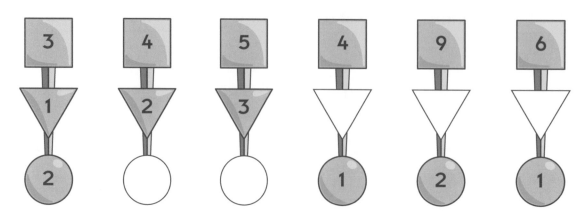

Dice puzzles

Equipment: dice

1 Add the number of spots on opposite faces of your die.
Check all the pairs of opposite faces. What have you found?

_____

Now place your die on the desk as shown in each question.

2

How many spots
are opposite:

a 2? _____

b 4? _____

3

How many spots
are opposite:

a 5? _____

b 1? _____

4

How many spots
are opposite:

a 6? _____

b 3? _____

5 Which of the dice below have something wrong?
Explain why to your teacher.

  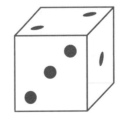

6 What is the sum of the spots
on the two faces that are joined? _____

How many spots on these faces? _____ _____

We can separate these two dice.

six spots
on this face

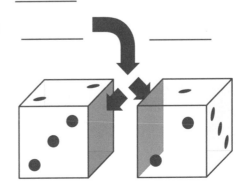

Who am I?

1 I am 5 more than 3. _____

2 I am 4 less than 10. _____

3 I am an even number.
I am more than 7 and less than 10. _____

4 I am an odd number less than 10.
I am more than 3 and less than 6. _____

5 I am an odd number.
I am 2 less than 9. _____

6 I am an odd number less than 20.
I am 5 less than 18. _____

7 I am more than 10.
I am less than 20.
You will find me if you count in 5s. _____

8 I am even. You will find me if you count in 10s.
I am less than 50.
I am more than 32. _____

9 I am odd. You will find me if you count in 5s.
I am less than 30.
I am more than 22. _____

10 I am even. You will find me if you count in 2s.
I am less than 17.
I am more than 14. _____

 Make up your own number problems
and ask friends or your parents to solve them.

Space arithmetic

If ■ + ■ = 6   and   ▲ − ■ = 5 then,

■ = 3   and   ▲ = 8

Find the value of each shape below.

1

□ + □ = 2

● + □ = 4

□ = _____

● = _____

2

▲ + ▲ + ▲ = 6

▲ + ● = 5

▲ = _____

● = _____

3

★ + ★ = 10

★ − ◗ = 4

★ = _____

◗ = _____

4

☆ + ☆ = 2

■ − ☆ = 2

☆ = _____

■ = _____

5

◗ + ◗ = 8

◗ − ▲ = 2

◗ = _____

▲ = _____

6

▲ + ▲ = 4

▲ + 🚀 = 6

▲ = _____

🚀 = _____

7

● + ● + ● = 15

▲ − ● = 2

● = _____

▲ = _____

8

🚀 + 🚀 = 14

◗ − 🚀 = 3

🚀 = _____

◗ = _____

9

★ + 🪐 = 6

★ − 🪐 = 2

★ = _____

🪐 = _____

Shape puzzles

Find the value of each shape in these puzzles.

1
△ + △ = 8
● + △ = 9

△ = _____   ● = _____

2
+ = 10
+ = 8

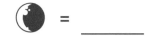
= _____   = _____

3
★ + ★ = 12
− ★ = 4

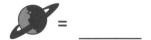
★ = _____   = _____

4
■ + ■ + ■ = 9
■ + 🪐 = 8

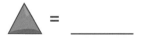
■ = _____   🪐 = _____

5
+ + = 6
△ − = 7

= _____   △ = _____

6
+ ★ = 7
− ★ = 3

= _____   ★ = _____

7
● + ■ = 9
● − ■ = 1

● = _____   ■ = _____

Find my rule

Find the rule between the IN numbers and the OUT numbers and write all the missing OUT numbers.

In the first question the rule is:
Add 2 to the IN number to get the OUT number.

1

IN:	6	11	1	8	2	5	9	10	4	Rule
OUT:	8	13	3	10						

2

IN:	6	11	3	8	2	5	9	10	4	Rule
OUT:	7	12	4	9						

3

IN:	6	11	1	8	2	5	9	10	4	Rule
OUT:	5	10	0	7						

4

IN:	4	5	2	7	6	11	1	8	3	Rule
OUT:	7	8	5	10						

5

IN:	2	5	9	10	4	7	6	11	13	Rule
OUT:	0	3	7	8						

6

IN:	6	11	1	8	2	5	9	10	4	Rule
OUT:	10	15	5	12						

7

IN:	6	3	8	5	9	10	4	7	11	Rule
OUT:	3	0	5	2						

8

IN:	5	9	10	4	7	6	3	1	8	Rule
OUT:	10	14	15	9						

Sum of digits

1   Place the digits 1, 2 and 3 in the boxes and find the sum.

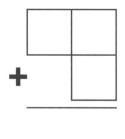

Can you place the digits in the boxes another way?

Place the digits 1, 2 and 3 in the boxes below in as many different ways as you can and find the sum in each case.

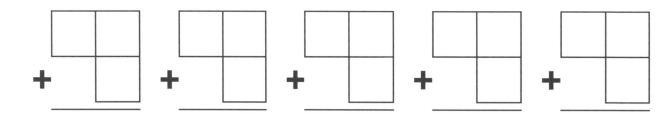

Draw a circle around the largest sum.
Draw a box around the smallest sum.

2   Place the digits 2, 3 and 4 in the boxes below so that you will find:

     a   the largest sum.   **b**   the smallest sum.

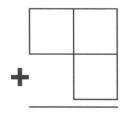 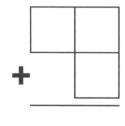

Number, Patterns & Algebra

Difference of digits

1   Place the digits 1, 2 and 3 in the
subtraction and find the difference.

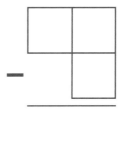

Can you place the digits in the boxes another way?

Place the digits in the boxes in as many different ways as you can
and find the difference in each case.

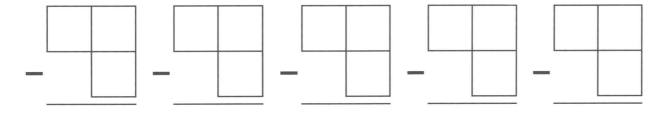

Draw a circle around the largest difference.
Draw a box around the smallest difference.

2   Place the digits 2, 3 and 4 in the boxes
below so that you will find:

   a   the largest difference.   **b**   the smallest difference.

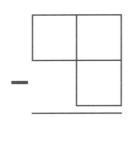 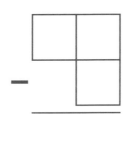 

Money

Which coins does each person use?

Draw a line joining each question to the correct answer in the box.

1 Rosemary buys a

 for 25c.

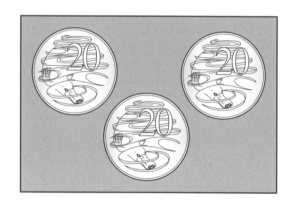

2 Jeremy buys a

 for 80c.

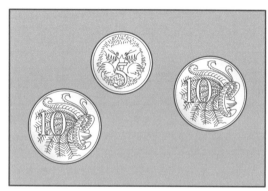

3 Ross buys a

for 60c.

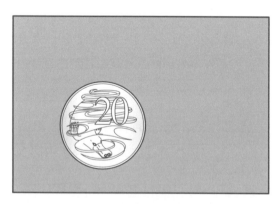

4 May buys a

for 20c.

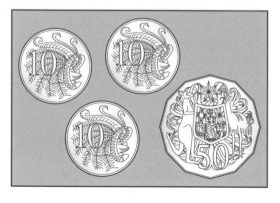

Shopping

What change does each person get?

Draw a line joining the question to the correct answer in the box.

1 Tanya has

and she buys a  for 25c.

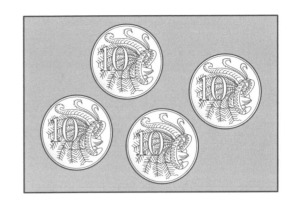

2 Gino has

and he buys a  for 80c.

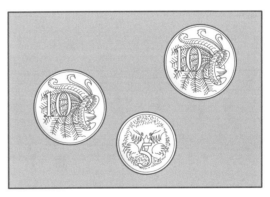

3 Linda has

and she buys a  for 60c.

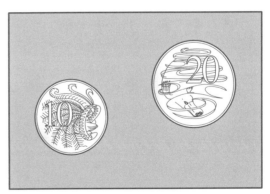

4 David has

and he buys a  for 20c.

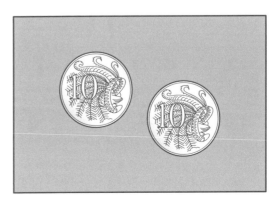

Patterns

Draw the next three shapes in each pattern.

1. ○ ○ — ○ ○ — ○ ○ — ____ ____ ____

2. ◆ ‖ ◆ ‖ ◆ ‖ ◆ ‖ ◆ ‖ ◆ ____ ____ ____

3. ◆ ● ● ◆ ● ● ◆ ● ● ____ ____ ____

4. \ \ ▮ \ \ ▮ \ \ ▮ ____ ____ ____

5. ▪ □ □ ▪ □ □ ▪ ____ ____ ____

6. ⁙ ★ ⁙ ★ ⁙ ★ ⁙ ★ ____ ____ ____

7. □ ● ▮ □ ● ▮ □ ● ▮ ____ ____ ____

8. ✛ ● ▮ ✛ ● ▮ ✛ ● ▮ ____ ____ ____

9. △ △ ◆ △ △ ◆ △ △ ◆ ____ ____ ____

10. △ ● △ ○ △ ● △ ○ △ ● △ ____ ____ ____

11. ■ ○ ■ ○ ○ ■ ○ ■ ○ ○ ____ ____ ____

12. △ ◆ ▮ △ ◆ ▮ △ ◆ ▮ ____ ____ ____

13. ◆ ⊕ ◆ ↓ ◆ ⊕ ◆ ↓ ◆ ⊕ ____ ____ ____

14. ▮ ○ ◇ ▮ ○ ◇ ▮ ○ ◇ ▮ ○ ◇ ____ ____ ____

Tile patterns

Equipment: square tiles

Make these patterns using your square tiles and then draw the next picture in each pattern.

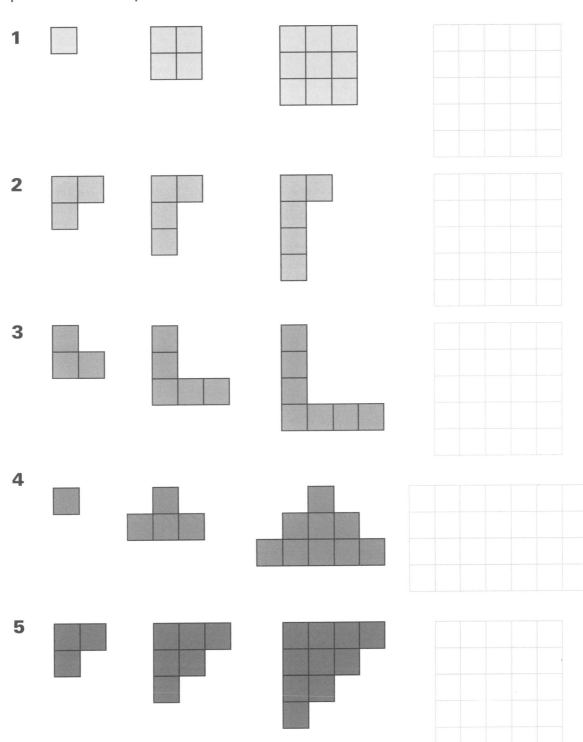

Square tiles

 Equipment: square tiles

To build a two-step staircase
I need three squares.

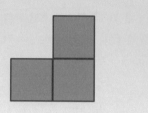

1 How many squares do I need
to build this three-step staircase? _____

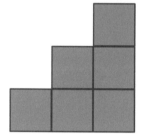

2 How many squares do I need
to build a four-step staircase? _____

Draw the diagram and count the squares.

3 If I use 15 squares, how many
steps are there in my staircase? _____

 Draw the diagram. You may need to use a separate page.

4 Can you find a pattern? Complete the table below.

Number of steps in staircase	Number of squares
2	3
3	
4	
5	
6	
7	

What's the chance?

Tick the box which best describes the chance that:

		impossible	certain	uncertain
1	I will go to school tomorrow.			
2	I will read a book today.			
3	I will swim today.			
4	It will rain today.			
5	I will play in the sand pit today.			
6	I will get a present today.			
7	I will walk home today.			
8	I will kiss my teacher tomorrow.			
9	My favourite toy will come to life overnight.			
10	It will snow today.			
11	My teacher will give me an award this week.			
12	I will not have breakfast tomorrow.			
13	I will sleep till 11 a.m. tomorrow.			
14	I will use a computer today.			
15	I will be as tall as my dad by next year.			
16	I will make my own lunch tomorrow.			

Shading blocks

1 Colour in one of the little squares in each block (the first one has been done for you). Each of the other three pictures should be different.

2 This time colour in two squares (the first one has been done for you). Remember, each picture should be different.

3 This time colour in three squares. Remember, each picture should be different.

4 How many other pictures can you make that are different from any of the above in questions 1, 2 or 3?

enrich-e-matics
3rd EDITION
BOOK 1
ANSWERS

Total of ten (page 1)

1	2	3	4	5	6	7	8	9	10

Total of twelve (page 2)

1	2	3	4	5	6	7	8	9	10

Number sentences (page 3)

1 1	**2** 2	**3** 5	**4** 4	**5** 5
6 1	**7** 4	**8** 3	**9** 4	**10** 5
11 2	**12** 3	**13** 4	**14** 5	

Add or subtract (page 4)

1 +	**2** –	**3** –	**4** +
5 –	**6** +	**7** –	**8** –
9 +	**10** –	**11** –	**12** +
13 +	**14** –	**15** +	**16** –

Number patterns (page 5)

1 13, 15	**2** 13, 16	**3** 7, 5	**4** 12, 14
5 25, 30	**6** 50, 60	**7** 50, 40	**8** 43, 53
9 55, 66	**10** 16, 14		

What comes next? (page 6)

1 24, 27	**2** 15, 18	**3** 14, 13	**4** 44, 33
5 13, 11	**6** 15, 10	**7** 51, 61	**8** 44, 54
9 11, 8	**10** 30, 32	**11** 20, 15	**12** 22, 20
13 47, 37	**14** 17, 21		

Continue the pattern (page 7)

1 8642 8642 8642	**2** 12345 12345
3 357 99 357 99	**4** 1223 1223 1223
5 9876 9876 9876	**6** 2468 2468 2468
7 30 220 30 220	**8** 7339 7339 7339
9 5445 5445 5445	**10** 97579 97579
11 5311 5311 5311	**12** 123 321 123 321

Bricks (page 8)

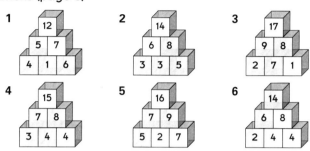

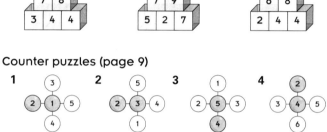

Counter puzzles (page 9)

The 3 and 4 can be interchanged.

The 1 and 5 can be interchanged.

The 2 and 3 can be interchanged.

The 3 and 5 can be interchanged.

What number fits? (page 10)

1 The 6 and 4 can be interchanged.

2 The 6 and 3 can be interchanged.

3 The 3 and 6 can be interchanged, or the 4 and 5 can be interchanged, and 3 and 6 can be swapped with 4 and 5.

4 The 2 and 5 can be interchanged, or the 4 and 3 can be interchanged, and 2 and 5 can be swapped with 4 and 3.

A

Difference of digits (page35)

1
$$12 - 3 = 9$$ $$13 - 2 = 11$$ $$21 - 3 = 18$$ $$23 - 1 = 22$$ $$31 - 2 = 29$$ $$32 - 1 = 31$$

2 a $43 - 2 = 41$ **b** $23 - 4 = 19$

Money (page 36)

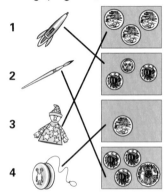

Shopping (page 37)

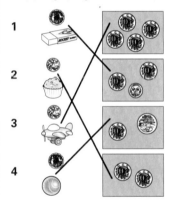

Patterns (page 38)

1   **2**   **3**   **4**

5   **6**   **7**   **8**

9 ... **10** ... **11** **12** ...

13   **14**

Tile patterns (page 39)

1   **2**   **3**

4   **5**

Square tiles (page 40)

1 6 **2** 10   **3** 5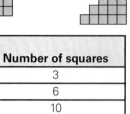

4

Number of steps in staircase	Number of squares
2	3
3	6
4	10
5	15
6	21
7	28

What's the chance? (page 41)

Answers will vary and need careful discussion to ensure that children understand the concept of 'impossible', 'certain' and 'uncertain'.

Shading blocks (page 42)

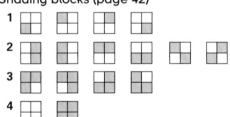

Different shading (page 43)

Flag patterns (page 44)

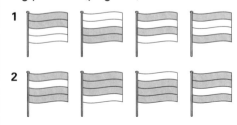

How many apples? (page 25)

1 8 **2** 20 **3** 6 **4** 8 **5** 15 **6** 24

Number line (page 26)

1 3 **2** 4 **3** 4 **4** 6 **5** 4 **6** 12
7 20 **8** 12 **9** 10 **10** 6 **11** 2 **12** 20

Bowling pins (page 27)

1 a 2 and 7 **b** 3 and 9 or 4 and 8

2 a 2 and 3 and 7 **b** 2 and 4 and 8 or 3 and 4 and 7

3 a 6 and 5 or 3 and 8 **b** 6 and 7 or 8 and 5 or 9 and 4

4 a 4 and 5 and 6 or 5 and 3 and 7

   b 3 and 6 and 8 or 4 and 5 and 8
     or 4 and 6 and 7 or 3 and 5 and 9

5 4 and 6 and 3 and 7 or 3 and 4 and 5 and 8

Missing numbers (page 28)

1 5, 8, 4, 3, 3, 6, 4, 3, 2, 4, 6 **2** 2, 2, 3, 7, 5

Dice puzzles (page 29)

1 The spots on opposite faces add to 7.

2 a 5 **b** 3
3 a 2 **b** 6
4 a 1 **b** 4

5 First die: 5 and 2 should be on opposite faces.
Second die: 4 and 3 should be on opposite faces.

6 5 is the sum; 1 spot, 4 spots

Who am I? (page 30)

1 8 **2** 6 **3** 8 **4** 5 **5** 7
6 13 **7** 15 **8** 40 **9** 25 **10** 16

Space arithmetic (page 31)

1 ▢ = 1, ◯ = 3
2 △ = 2, ◯ = 3
3 ★ = 5, ◐ = 1

4 ☆ = 1, ▢ = 3
5 ◐ = 4, △ = 2
6 △ = 2, ⬗ = 4

7 ◯ = 5, △ = 7
8 ⬠ = 7, ◐ = 10
9 ☆ = 4, ◉ = 2

Shape puzzles (page 32)

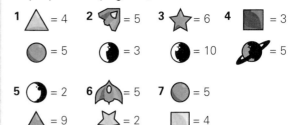

1 △ = 4 **2** = 5 **3** ★ = 6 **4** ▢ = 3

◯ = 5 ◐ = 3 ◐ = 10 ◉ = 5

5 ◐ = 2 **6** = 5 **7** ◯ = 5

△ = 9 ☆ = 2 ▢ = 4

Find my rule (page 33)

1

IN:	6	11	1	8	2	5	9	10	4	Rule
OUT:	8	13	3	10	**4**	**7**	**11**	**12**	6	**+ 2**

2

IN:	6	11	3	8	2	5	9	10	4	Rule
OUT:	7	12	4	9	**3**	**6**	**10**	**11**	5	**+ 1**

3

IN:	6	11	1	8	2	5	9	10	4	Rule
OUT:	5	10	0	7	**1**	**4**	**8**	**9**	3	**− 1**

4

IN:	4	5	2	7	6	11	1	8	3	Rule
OUT:	7	8	5	10	**9**	**14**	**4**	**11**	6	**+ 3**

5

IN:	2	5	9	10	4	7	6	11	13	Rule
OUT:	0	3	7	8	**2**	**5**	**4**	**9**	11	**− 2**

6

IN:	6	11	1	8	2	5	9	10	4	Rule
OUT:	10	15	5	12	**6**	**9**	**13**	**14**	8	**+ 4**

7

IN:	6	3	8	5	9	10	4	7	11	Rule
OUT:	3	0	5	2	**6**	**7**	**1**	**4**	8	**− 3**

8

IN:	5	9	10	4	7	6	3	1	8	Rule
OUT:	10	14	15	9	**12**	**11**	**8**	**6**	13	**+ 5**

Sum of digits (page 34)

1

```
 12      13      21
+ 3     + 2     + 3
────    ────    ────
 15      15      24
```

```
 23      31      32
+ 1     + 2     + 1
────    ────    ────
 24      33      33
```

The largest sum is 33.
The smallest sum is 15.

2 a

```
 43   or   42
+ 2       + 3
────      ────
 45        45
```

b

```
 23   or   24
+ 4       + 3
────      ────
 27        27
```

The largest difference is 31.
The smallest difference is 9

Place the numbers (page 11)

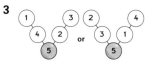

1
2 — 1 — 5   3 — 1 — 4   or
3   5
4   2

2 and 5 or 3 and 4 can be swapped.

2
1 — 3 — 5   2 — 3 — 4   or
2   1
4   5

1 and 5 or 2 and 4 can be swapped.

3
1 — 3   2 — 4   or
4 — 2   3 — 1
5   5

1 and 4 or 3 and 2 can be swapped.

4
5 — 2
1
4 — 3

Numbers in circles (page 12)

1 6 1 / 5 2 / 4 3

2 2 / 1 5 4 / 3

3 5 / 3 1 / 4 2 6

Numbers in triangles (page 13)

1 1 / 6 5 / 2 4 3

2 5 / 3 1 / 4 2 6

3 3 / 2 1 / 4 — 5

4 1 / 6 4 / 3 2 5

Abacus numbers (page 14)

1 13	**2** 4	**3** 11	**4** 22	**5** 15
6 20	**7** 24	**8** 34	**9** 31	

Which abacus number? (page 15)

1 25	**2** 6	**3** 12	**4** 44	**5** 18
6 50	**7** 51	**8** 43	**9** 37	

Abacus addition (page 16)

1 12, 13 or 22	**2** 4, 5 or 14	**3** 11, 12 or 21
4 22, 23 or 32	**5** 15, 16 or 25	**6** 20, 21 or 30

Abacus subtraction (page 17)

1 12, 11 or 2	**2** 15, 14 or 5	**3** 11, 10 or 1
4 22, 21 or 12	**5** 34, 33 or 24	**6** 24, 23 or 14

Abacus challenge (page 18)

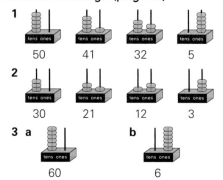

1   50   41   32   5

2   30   21   12   3

3 a 60   **b** 6

Grid sums (page 19)

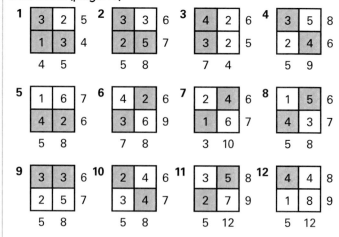

1
| 3 | 2 | 5 |
| 1 | 3 | 4 |
4   5

2
| 3 | 3 | 6 |
| 2 | 5 | 7 |
5   8

3
| 4 | 2 | 6 |
| 3 | 2 | 5 |
7   4

4
| 3 | 5 | 8 |
| 2 | 4 | 6 |
5   9

5
| 1 | 6 | 7 |
| 4 | 2 | 6 |
5   8

6
| 4 | 2 | 6 |
| 3 | 6 | 9 |
7   8

7
| 2 | 4 | 6 |
| 1 | 6 | 7 |
3   10

8
| 1 | 5 | 6 |
| 4 | 3 | 7 |
5   8

9
| 3 | 3 | 6 |
| 2 | 5 | 7 |
5   8

10
| 2 | 4 | 6 |
| 3 | 4 | 7 |
5   8

11
| 3 | 5 | 8 |
| 2 | 7 | 9 |
5   12

12
| 4 | 4 | 8 |
| 1 | 8 | 9 |
5   12

Find my start (page 20)

1	8
2	12
3	8
4	12
5	22
6	6
7	4

Parts of shapes (page 21)

1 2, 8	**2** 2, 6	**3** 4, 5	**4** 3, 6	**5** 4, 9
6 4, 8	**7** 2, 4	**8** 6, 12	**9** 4, 6	

Fractions (page 22)

Tick 1, 2, 4, 5 and 6.   Colour 3 and 7.

Find the value (page 23)

1 16c	**2** 9c	**3** 40c	**4** 44c	**5** 20c	**6** 12c
7 20c	**8** 60c	**9** 60c	**10** 28c	**11** 60c	**12** 24c

Halves and quarters (page 24)

1 4	**2** 10	**3** 14	**4** 8	**5** 12	**6** 20

Tessellations (page 74)

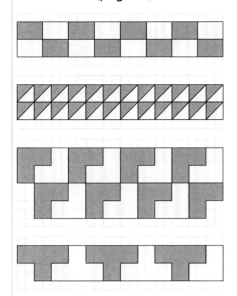

Spatial reasoning (page 75)

1	**2**	**3**	**4**
5	**6**	**7**	**8**
9	**10**	**11**	**12**
13	**14**	**15**	**16**
17	**18**	**19**	**20**

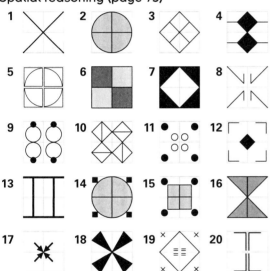

Shapes and values (page 76)

1 = 2

2 = 2
= 3

3 = 4
= 1

4 = 2
= 5

5 = 7
= 4

6 = 5
= 3

7 = 10
= 5

8 = 6
= 1

9 = 8
= 9

Odd one out (page 77)

1 C   **2** C   **3** B   **4** B   **5** C   **6** A

Complete the picture (page 78)

1   **2**   **3**   **4**   **5**

How many squares? (page 79)

1 9	**2** 10	**3** 12	**4** 15	**5** 11
6 15	**7** 12	**8** 13	**9** 12	

Shading halves (page 80)

There are many possible solutions. These are some of them.

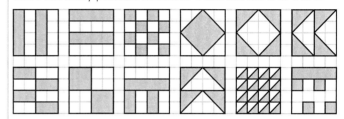

Drawing lines (page 81)

There are many possible solutions. These are some of them.

1 or   **2** or or

3 a or or   **b** or

No threes (page 82)

Not all possibilities are listed and it is not expected that students find more than two solutions.

1   **2**

3

G

What day? (page 57)
1 a Thursday **b** Tuesday **c** Saturday **d** Wednesday
2 a Sunday **b** Friday **c** Tuesday **d** Saturday
3 a Wednesday **b** Saturday **c** Monday **d** Monday

May days (page 58)
1 Saturday **2** 4 **3** 4 **4** Thursday
5 Wednesday **6** Thursday **7** 31 **8** No

Check the calendar (page 59)
1 31 **2** 4 **3** 5 **4** Monday
5 Monday **6** Thursday **7** Thursday **8** 18 days
9 16 days **10** 4

Scales (pages 60 and 61)
1 1 kg **2** 5 kg **3** 10 kg **4** 3 kg **5** 8 kg
6 9 kg **7** 5 kg **8** 10 kg **9** 14 kg **10** 4 kg
11 7 kg **12** 3 kg **13** 13 kg **14** 7 kg

Perimeter (page 62)
1 10 cm **2** 12 cm **3** 16 cm **4** 16 cm **5** 16 cm
6 14 cm **7** 18 cm **8** 14 cm **9** 16 cm

Temperature facts? (page 63)
1 False **2** True **3** False **4** False
5 True **6** False **7** True **8** False
9 True **10** True **11** False **12** False

Measurement facts? (page 64)
1 False **2** False **3** False **4** True **5** False
6 True **7** True **8** True **9** False **10** False
11 True **12** True **13** True **14** False **15** True

Building blocks (page 65)
1 4, 5, 8 **2** 6, 9, 10 **3** 7, 11, 12

Moving blocks (page 66)
1 5, 6, 8 **2** 4, 9, 10 **3** 7, 11, 12

Enlarging figures (page 67)

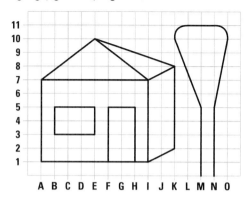

Same shapes (page 68)
1, 14 2, 19 3, 11 4, 20 5, 25
6, 15 7, 26 8, 21 9, 22 10, 23
12, 18 13, 16 17, 24

Combining shapes (page 69)

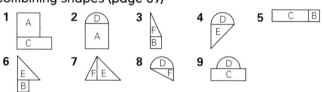

Making triangles (page 70)
1 ◿◿◿◿ **2** 12 **3** ◿◿◿◿◿
4 15 **5** 18 ◿◿◿◿◿◿◿

Making squares (page 71)
1 ☐☐☐☐ **2** 13 **3** ☐☐☐☐☐
4 16 **5** 19 ☐☐☐☐☐☐

In a line (page 72)
1 a 2 **b** 5 **c** 11
2 a 5 **b** 6 **c** 7

Match the objects (page 73)

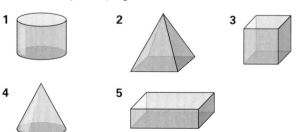

Shading circles (page 45)

Picture graphs (page 46)

1

month	picture	rainfall
May	🌢🌢🌢	6 mm
June	🌢🌢🌢🌢	8 mm
July	🌢🌢	4 mm
August	🌢🌢🌢🌢🌢🌢	12 mm

2

month	picture	rainfall
September	🌢	2 mm
October	🌢🌢🌢🌢🌢	10 mm
November	🌢🌢🌢🌢	8 mm
December	🌢🌢	4 mm

Birthday graphs (page 47)

1

month	picture	number of children
January	👤👤👤	9
February	👤👤	6
March	👤👤👤👤	12
April	👤👤👤👤👤	15
May	👤👤👤👤👤👤👤	21

2 May   **3** February   **4** 63

Favourite subjects (page 48)

1 6   **2** 4   **3** Computing
4 Sport   **5** Maths and Music   **6** 2

Weather (page 49)

1 True   **2** False   **3** True
4 False   **5** True   **6** True

Test results (page 50)

1 6   **2** 7   **3** 2   **4** 2
5

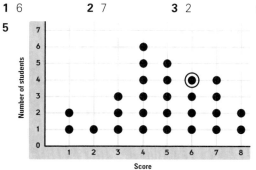

6 27 including students who did it late   **7** 6   **8** 6

Class captain (page 51)

1 a Tom   **b** Lee   **c** Josh   **d** Ann   **e** Emma
2 35
3

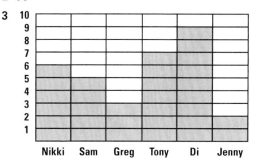

How long? (page 52)

1 4   **2** 2   **3** 6   **4** 3
5 8   **6** 6   **7** 12   **8** 10

Measure the rocket (page 53)

1 3   **2** 4   **3** 6   **4** 4
5 40   **6** 50   **7** 8   **8** 10

Long or short? (page 54)

1 8   **2** 20   **3** 12   **4** 12
5 15   **6** 8   **7** 15   **8** 6

Find the temperature (page 55)

1 10°C   **2** 20°C   **3** 40°C   **4** 8°C   **5** 35°C
6 9°C   **7** 25°C   **8** 15°C   **9** 7°C   **10** 30°C

Time (page 56)

1 4 p.m.   **2** 7 p.m.   **3** 5 p.m.   **4** 1 p.m.
5 2 p.m.   **6** 10 p.m.   **7** 9 p.m.   **8** 4 p.m.
9 5 p.m.   **10** 9 p.m.   **11** 2 p.m.   **12** 12 noon
13 11 a.m.   **14** 8 a.m.

Balancing act (page 83)

1

2

3

4

5

6

Balance (page 84)

1

2

3

4

5

6

Find your balance (page 85)

1 8 **2** 6 **3** 11 **4** 7
5 5 **6** 4 **7** 1

Number of pins? (page 86)

1 a 8 **b** 10
2 a 7 **b** 9
3 a 6 **b** 7

Grid puzzles (page 87)

1 **2** **3**

4 **5** **6**

Gridlock (page 88)

1 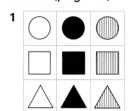 **2**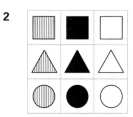

3 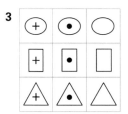 **4**

5 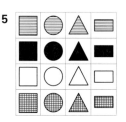 **6**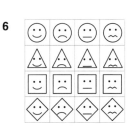

H

Different shading

If we had to shade 2 squares out of these 3 squares, we could do it in 3 different ways. Study these carefully.

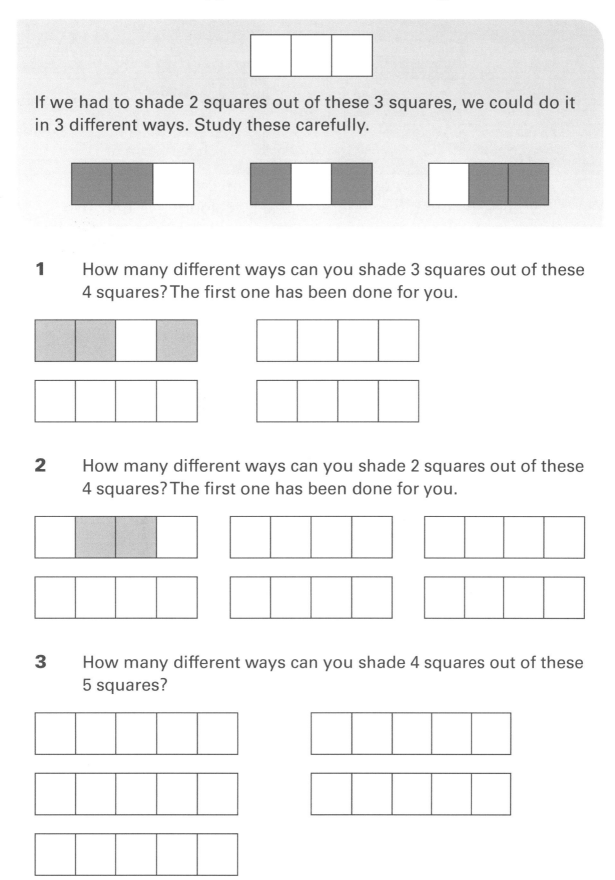

1 How many different ways can you shade 3 squares out of these 4 squares? The first one has been done for you.

2 How many different ways can you shade 2 squares out of these 4 squares? The first one has been done for you.

3 How many different ways can you shade 4 squares out of these 5 squares?

Flag patterns

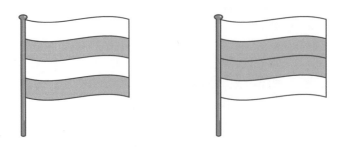

1 In these flags only two of the stripes are coloured in. Can you make four other different flags by colouring in only two stripes?

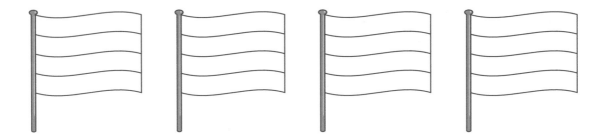

2 How many different flags can you make by colouring in three stripes? The first is done for you.

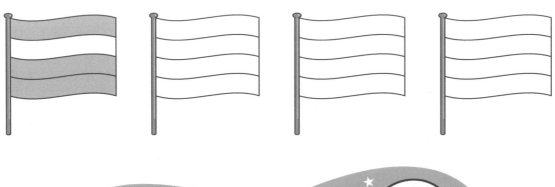

Shading circles

A circle like this can be shaded in four different ways using two colours.

In how many different ways can you shade a circle like this using two different colours?

Try to work systematically. First shade only one sector or part with a coloured pencil in all three different positions.

For the next three diagrams shade two sectors or parts with the same coloured pencil in all three different positions.

Now use your second coloured pencil to shade the white sectors in the six circles above. There are two more shadings that you have not done. Complete these.

Now check carefully that all your shadings are complete and different.

Picture graphs

Chance & Data

If 💧 represents 2 mm of rain, then 💧 💧 💧 represents 6 mm of rain.

Complete each table below.

1   How many centimetres of rain fell in each month?

month	picture	rainfall
May	💧 💧 💧	6 mm
June	💧 💧 💧 💧	
July	💧 💧	
August	💧 💧 💧 💧 💧 💧	

2   Draw pictures in the table below to show rainfall.

One 💧 represents 2 mm of rain.

month	picture	rainfall
September		2 mm
October		10 mm
November		8 mm
December		4 mm

Birthday graphs

In a school, all year 1 and 2 students were asked in which month they had their birthday. A picture graph was drawn so that ☺ represented three children.

This picture graph shows the first five months only.

1 Complete the table below.

month	picture	number of children
January	☺ ☺ ☺	9
February	☺ ☺	
March	☺ ☺ ☺ ☺	
April		15
May		21

2 In which month did most children have their birthday? _____

3 In which month did the least number of children have their birthday? _____

4 How many children altogether had their birthdays in these five months? _____

Favourite subjects

Ten (10) children were asked which lessons they enjoyed at school.

This table shows that 8 children enjoy Maths at school.

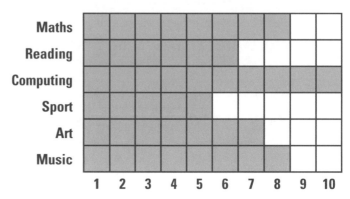

1 How many children enjoy reading at school? _____

2 How many children do not like reading at school? _____

3 Which subject do all children like? _____

4 Which subject is liked by the
smallest number of children? _____

5 Which subjects did the
same number of children enjoy? _____

6 How many children do not enjoy music? _____

Use this graph to colour one rectangle for each subject
that you like at school.

Now choose 9 friends.
Ask them which
subjects they like at
school. Colour in the
rectangles for each
subject that they enjoy.

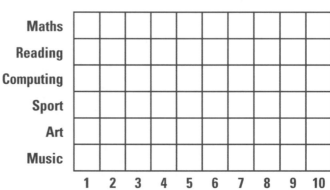

Weather

Using the table, colour in either the 'true' or 'false' bubble after each statement.

	week 1	week 2	week 3	week 4
Monday	cloudy	sunny	sunny	rainy
Tuesday	cloudy	sunny	cloudy	sunny
Wednesday	sunny	rainy	cloudy	sunny
Thursday	rainy	rainy	rainy	cloudy
Friday	sunny	rainy	rainy	sunny
Saturday	sunny	rainy	rainy	rainy
Sunday	sunny	rainy	cloudy	cloudy

sunny	cloudy	rainy

		True	False
1	Week 2 had five rainy days.	◯	◯
2	Week 4 had the most sunny days.	◯	◯
3	Weeks 1 and 4 had the same number of cloudy days.	◯	◯
4	For these four weeks it rained every Thursday.	◯	◯
5	Week 3 only had one sunny day.	◯	◯
6	Week 3 had three cloudy days.	◯	◯

Test results

The graph below shows students' marks in a Maths test out of 8.

Two students only got a score of 1.

Three students got a score of 6.

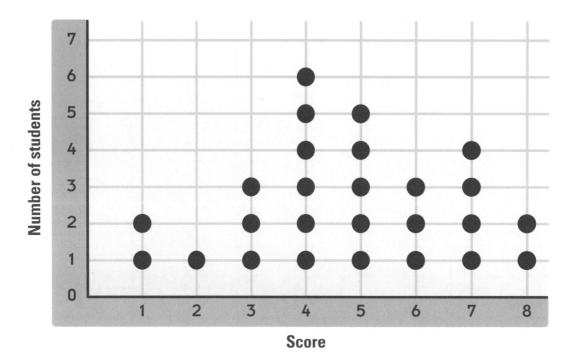

1   How many students got a score of 4? _____

2   Four students got the same score. What score was this? _____

3   How many students got the highest score? _____

4   Only one person got this score. What score was it? _____

5   One person was away sick, and when she did the
test she got 6. Add this extra mark on your graph.

6   How many students did this test altogether? _____

7   How many students got a score of more than 6? _____

8   How many students got a score of less than 4? _____

Class captain

1. This graph shows the result of a class election for class captain. Use the graph to work out who I am.

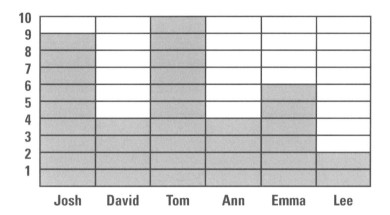

a   I have the most votes and won the election. _____

b   I have the least votes. _____

c   I came second in the election. _____

d   I have the same number of votes as David. _____

e   I have 6 votes. _____

2. How many people voted in the class election in the above question? _____

3. In another class the results of the class election were as follows:

Person	Number of votes
Nikki	6
Sam	5
Greg	3
Tony	7
Di	9
Jenny	2

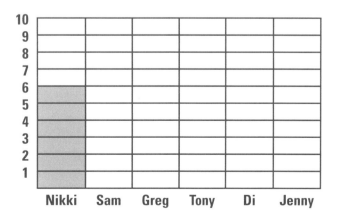

Show this information on this graph by colouring in the correct number of boxes for each person. The first one has been done for you.

How long?

The length of this rocket is 5 cm.

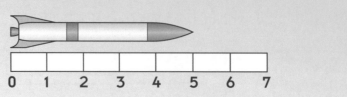

The length of each rocket below is:

1 _____ cm

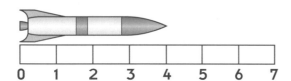

2 _____ cm

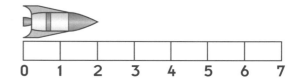

3 _____ cm

4 _____ cm

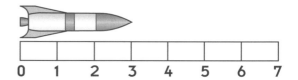

5 _____ cm

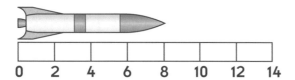

6 _____ cm

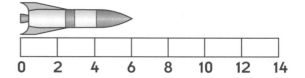

7 _____ cm

8 _____ cm

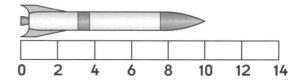

52

Measure the rocket

The length of this rocket is 5 cm.   The length of this rocket is 3 cm.

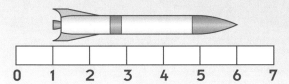 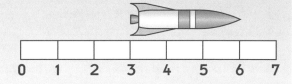

The length of each rocket below is:

1 _____ cm

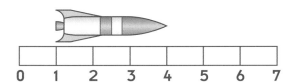

2 _____ cm

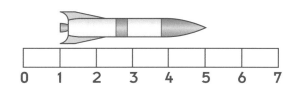

3 _____ cm

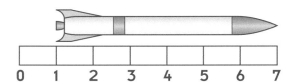

4 _____ cm

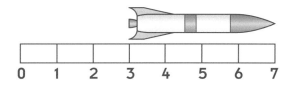

5 _____ cm

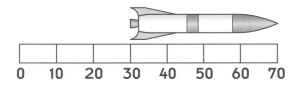

6 _____ cm

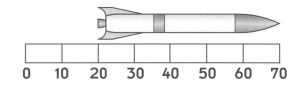

7 _____ cm

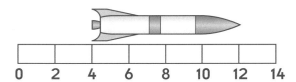

8 _____ cm

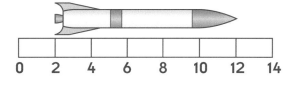

Long or short?

The length of this rocket is 5 cm.   The length of this rocket is 25 cm.

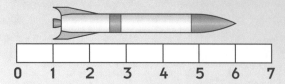
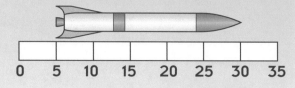

The length of each rocket below is:

1 _____ cm

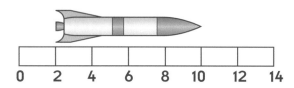

2 _____ cm

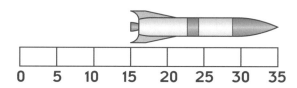

3 _____ cm

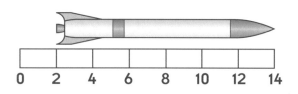

4 _____ cm

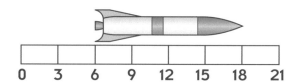

5 _____ cm

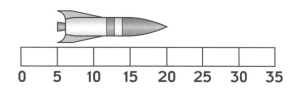

6 _____ cm

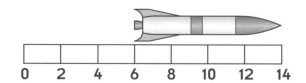

7 _____ cm

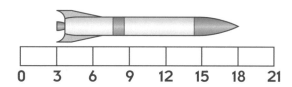

8 _____ cm

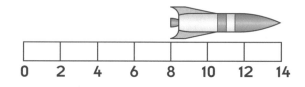

Find the temperature

Find the temperature shown on each thermometer.
All measurements are in °C.

Look carefully at the scale on each one first.

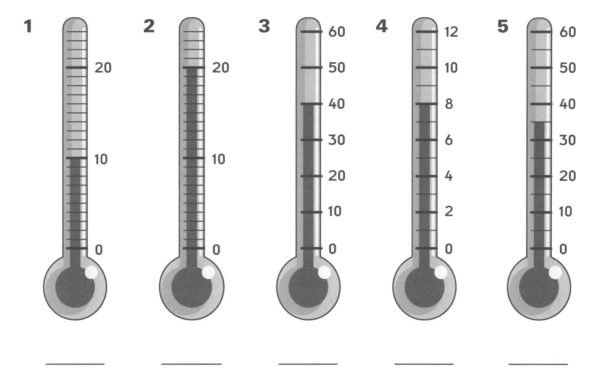

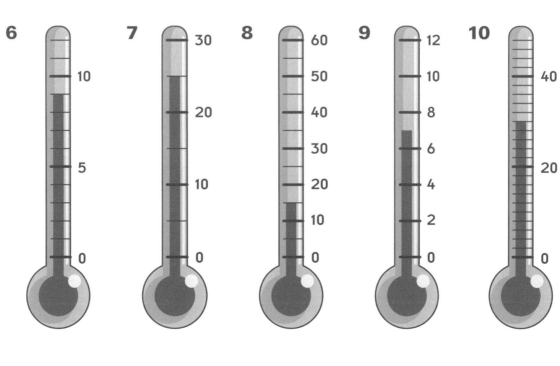

Time

What is the time:

1   2 hours after 2 p.m.? _____

2   5 hours after 2 p.m.? _____

3   3 hours after 2 p.m.? _____

4   1 hour before 2 p.m.? _____

5   5 hours before 7 p.m.? _____

6   3 hours after 7 p.m.? _____

7   2 hours after 7 p.m.? _____

8   3 hours before 7 p.m.? _____

9   5 hours after 12 noon? _____

10   9 hours after 12 noon? _____

11   3 hours before 5 p.m.? _____

12   4 hours before 4 p.m.? _____

13   4 hours before 3 p.m.? _____

14   6 hours before 2 p.m.? _____

What day?

The days of the week are: Monday, Tuesday, Wednesday, Thursday, Friday, Saturday and Sunday. Remember that there are seven days in a week.

1 If today is Wednesday,

    a what day of the week will it be tomorrow? _____

    b what day of the week was it yesterday? _____

    c what day of the week
       will it be 3 days from now? _____

    d what day of the week
       will it be 7 days from now? _____

2 If today is Saturday,

    a what day of the week will it be tomorrow? _____

    b what day of the week was it yesterday? _____

    c what day of the week
       will it be 3 days from now? _____

    d what day of the week
       will it be 7 days from now? _____

3 If today is Monday,

    a what day of the week
       will it be the day after tomorrow? _____

    b what day of the week
       was it the day before yesterday? _____

    c what day of the week
       will it be 7 days from now? _____

    d what day of the week
       will it be 14 days from now? _____

May days

May						
S	**M**	**T**	**W**	**T**	**F**	**S**
			1	2	3	4
5	6	7	8	9	10	11
12	13	14	15	16	17	18
19	20	21	22	23	24	25
26	27	28	29	30	31	

In this calendar the days of the week (Sunday, Monday, Tuesday, Wednesday, Thursday, Friday, Saturday) are written as S, M, T, W, T, F, S in this order.

1 What day is 11 May? _____

2 Can you see that there are 5 Wednesdays in May? How many Sundays in May? _____

3 How many Saturdays in May? _____

4 What day is 30 May? _____

5 What day is it 1 day before 30 May? _____

6 What day is it 7 days after 9 May? _____

7 How many days has the month of May?

_____

8 Is it true that there are 5 Tuesdays in May?

_____

Check the calendar

June						
S	**M**	**T**	**W**	**T**	**F**	**S**
			1	2	3	4
5	6	7	8	9	10	11
12	13	14	15	16	17	18
19	20	21	22	23	24	25
26	27	28	29	30		

July						
S	**M**	**T**	**W**	**T**	**F**	**S**
					1	2
3	4	5	6	7	8	9
10	11	12	13	14	15	16
17	18	19	20	21	22	23
24	25	26	27	28	29	30
31						

In the calendar above, the days of the week (Sunday, Monday, Tuesday, Wednesday, Thursday, Friday, Saturday) are written as S, M, T, W, T, F, S in this order.

1 The calendar shows that there are 30 days in June. How many days in July? _____

2 Can you see that there are 5 Wednesdays in June? How many Sundays in June? _____

3 How many Sundays in July? _____

4 What day is 11 July? _____

5 What day is it 7 days before 11 July? _____

6 What day is 9 June? _____

7 What day is it 14 days after 9 June? _____

8 If the last day of term two is 24 June, how many school days in June? _____

9 If school holidays start on 25 June and end on 10 July, how many days are these holidays? _____

10 Bradley has a piano lesson every Thursday, except during the school holidays. How many piano lessons does he have in June? _____

Scales

The measurements are in kilograms on all these scales.

This scale shows 2 kg.

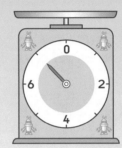

This scale shows 7 kg.

What weight does each of the following scales show?

It might help you to write in the missing numbers on each scale.

1

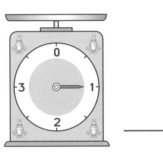

_____

2

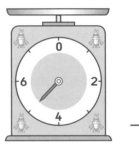

_____

3

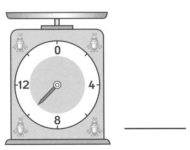

_____

4

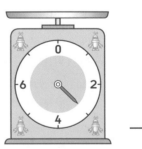

_____

5

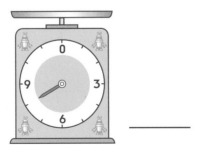

_____

6

_____

Scales continued

7

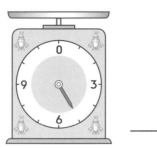

_____

8

_____

9

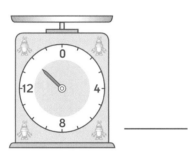

_____

10

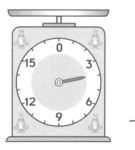

_____

11

_____

12

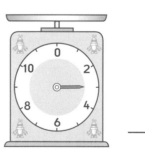

_____

13

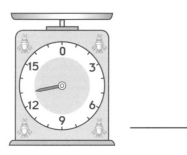

_____

14

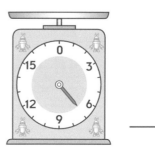

_____

Perimeter

The perimeter of a figure is the distance around its edge.

If the following is 1 cm grid paper, the perimeter of these three figures is shown. Check each one carefully. Pretend you are an ant walking along the outside of each figure.

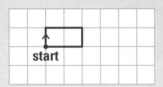

Perimeter
= 1+2+1+2
= 6 cm

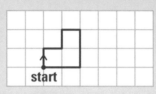

Perimeter
= 1+1+1+1+2+2
= 8 cm

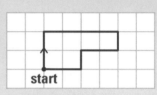

Perimeter
= 2+4+1+2+1+2
= 12 cm

Tim is an ant walking around these figures. For each question find how far he has walked and write down the perimeter of the figure. Write S where he starts.

1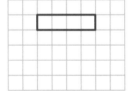

P = _____

2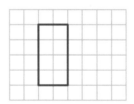

P = _____

3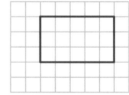

P = _____

4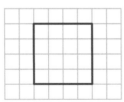

P = _____

5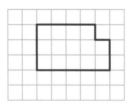

P = _____

6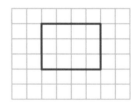

P = _____

7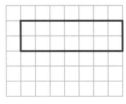

P = _____

8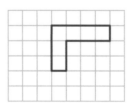

P = _____

9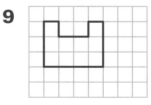

P = _____

Temperature facts?

Colour in either the 'true' or 'false' bubble for each statement, then discuss your answers with your teacher.

		True	False
1	The temperature of tap water is colder than the temperature of water from the fridge.	⬭	⬭
2	The temperature of ice cream is colder than the temperature of orange juice.	⬭	⬭
3	Boiling water comes out of the bathroom hot tap.	⬭	⬭
4	On a winter day the temperature is about 25°C.	⬭	⬭
5	An ice block melts at room temperature.	⬭	⬭
6	When a fresh cup of tea is left to stand, it gets hotter.	⬭	⬭
7	An ice cube will melt if you hold it in your hand.	⬭	⬭
8	The temperature of the water in an outdoor swimming pool is more than 37°C.	⬭	⬭
9	When it is 5°C we usually have a heater on.	⬭	⬭
10	When the temperature outside is 37°C we feel very hot.	⬭	⬭
11	When you are sick with fever your temperature is 36°C.	⬭	⬭
12	When it is snowing the temperature is about 10°C.	⬭	⬭

Measurement facts?

Colour in either the 'true' or 'false' bubble for each statement, then discuss your answers with your teacher.

		True	False
1	A glass of juice holds more than 1 litre.	◯	◯
2	Four spoonfuls of sugar will fill a cup.	◯	◯
3	I can drink 4 litres of water in 3 minutes if I am very thirsty.	◯	◯
4	The temperature is usually colder in the morning than it is in the middle of the day.	◯	◯
5	It takes about 10 seconds to blink.	◯	◯
6	September has 30 days.	◯	◯
7	In Australia most children are on holidays in January.	◯	◯
8	There are 7 days in a week.	◯	◯
9	It usually takes 1 hour to eat lunch at school.	◯	◯
10	Students usually get up at 9.30 a.m. on a school day.	◯	◯
11	At 1 a.m. most people are fast asleep.	◯	◯
12	Our classroom is smaller than our assembly hall.	◯	◯
13	There are 60 minutes in 1 hour.	◯	◯
14	There are 10 months in a year.	◯	◯
15	A soft drink bottle half full has more drink in it than when it is quarter full.	◯	◯

Building blocks

Liam built some shapes with his building blocks. When his sister Kim turned some of his shapes, she noticed that some were the same. Write down the numbers of the shapes that are the same as numbers 1, 2 and 3. You could build the shapes and experiment.

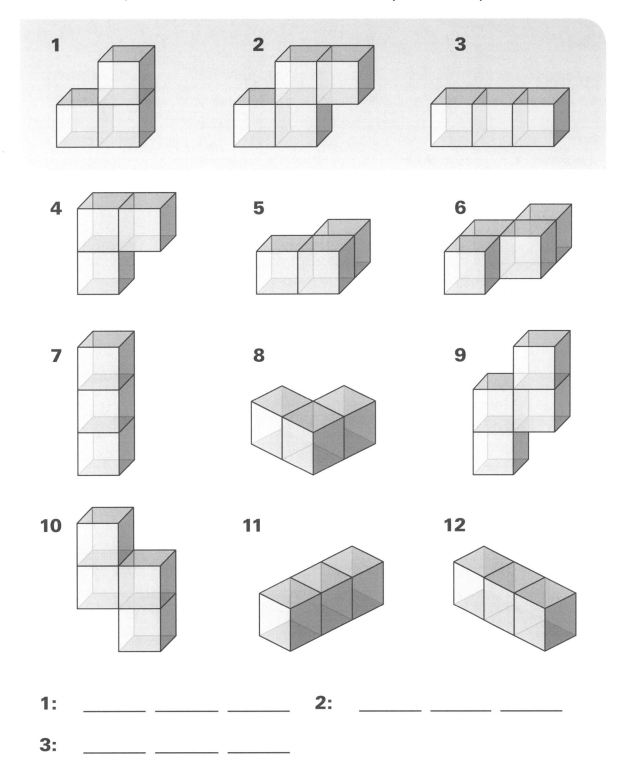

1: _____ _____ _____   2: _____ _____ _____

3: _____ _____ _____

Moving blocks

David built some shapes with his building blocks. When his sister Sarah turned some of his shapes, she noticed that some were the same. Write down the numbers of the shapes that are the same as 1, 2 or 3. Build the shapes and experiment.

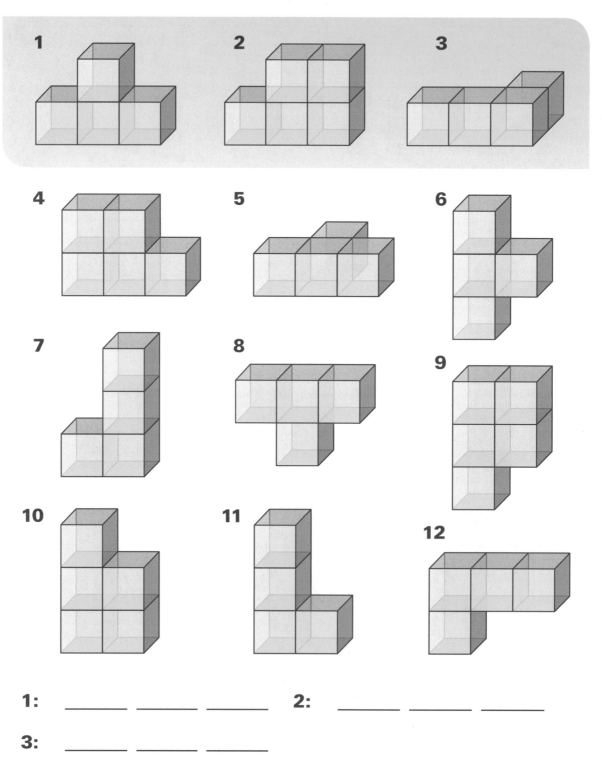

1: _____ _____ _____   2: _____ _____ _____

3: _____ _____ _____

Enlarging figures

Copy this figure carefully on the larger squared paper below.
It has been started for you.

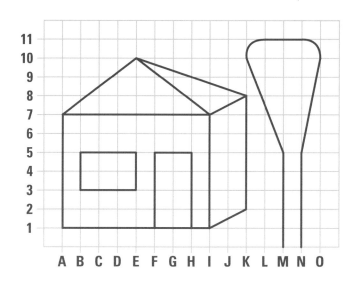

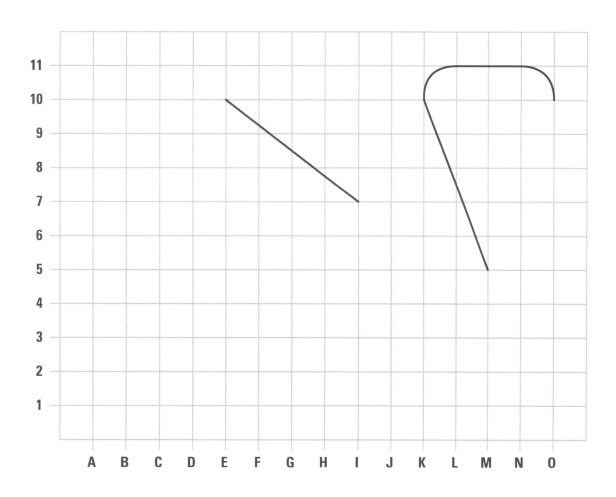

Same shapes

Colour in the two shapes that are the same. Use different colours for each pair of shapes.

Be careful as some of the shapes have been flipped or rotated.

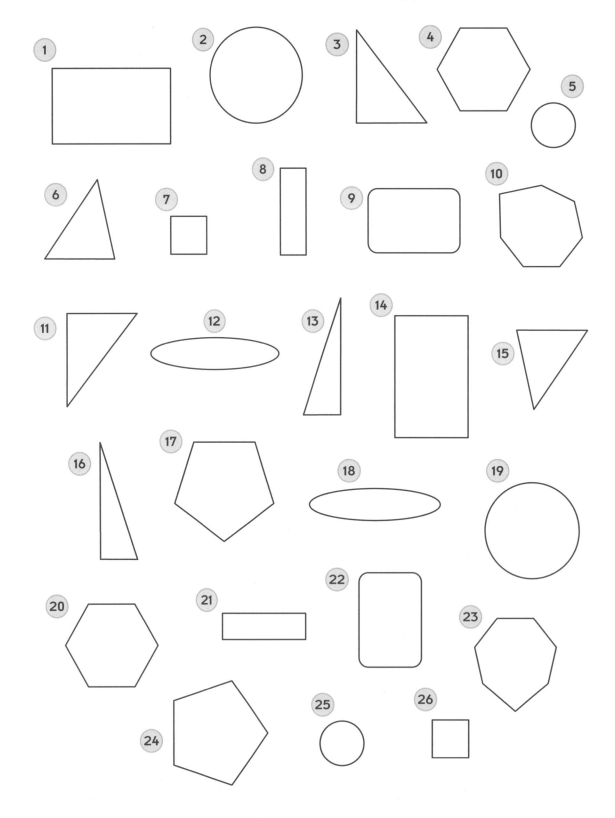

Combining shapes

Tess had the following building blocks.

On each diagram below, write the letters of the blocks used to build the shape. Drawing lines for the shapes might help.

This one is done for you.

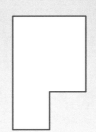

1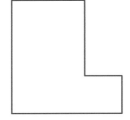

2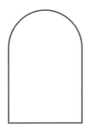

3

4

5

6

7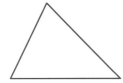

8

9

Making triangles

Three sticks are used to make this diagram of one triangle.

Six sticks are used to make this diagram of two triangles.

Nine sticks are used to make this diagram of three triangles.

1   Draw the diagram with four triangles.

2   How many sticks are used? _____

3   Draw the diagram with five triangles.

4   How many sticks are used? _____

5   How many sticks are used in a diagram with six triangles? _____

space

Making squares

Four sticks are used to make the diagram with one square.

Seven sticks are used to make the diagram with two squares.

Ten sticks are used to make the diagram with three squares.

1   Draw the diagram with four squares.

2   How many sticks are used? _____

3   Draw the diagram with five squares.

4   How many sticks are used? _____

5   How many sticks are used in a diagram with six squares? _____

In a line

If Paul (**X**) is 2nd from the front and 3rd from the back, then, there is one person in front of Paul and two people behind him.

There are four people in this line.

O

X

O

O

Draw a clear picture for each of these problems.

1 How many children are in front of Elizabeth if:

    a she is 3rd in line? _____

    b she is 6th in line? _____

    c she is 12th in line? _____

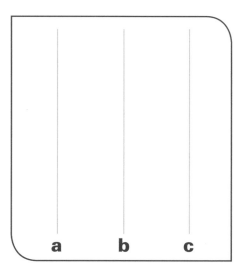

        a   **b**   **c**

2 Joseph is standing in a line waiting to buy lunch. How many children are there in the line if:

    a he is 3rd from the front and 3rd from the back? _____

    b he is 2nd from the front and 5th from the back? _____

    c he is 4th from the front and 4th from the back? _____

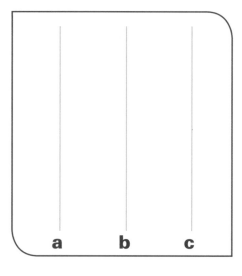

        a   **b**   **c**

Space

Match the objects

Given the clues below, draw a line from the dot to the matching object.

1 I have 2 circular faces.
I have a curved face.
Tins of baked beans
often look like me. ○

2 I have 5 faces, 4 are triangular
and 1 face is a square.
I have 8 edges.
I have 5 corners. ○

3 I have 6 square faces.
I have 12 edges.
Dice look like me. ○

4 I have 1 circular face.
I have a curved face. ○
I have 1 corner.
Ice cream cones look like me.

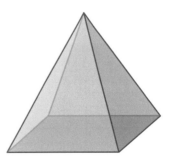

5 I have 6 rectangular faces.
I have 12 edges.
Boxes look like me. ○

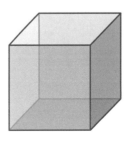

Tessellations

A tessellation is formed by repeating one or more shapes in such a way that they fit together without leaving gaps or overlapping.

Continue each tessellation below.

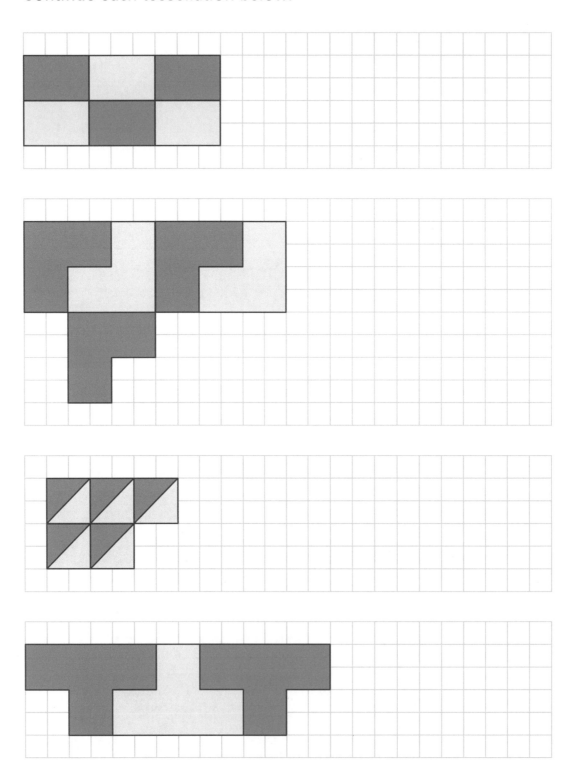

Spatial reasoning

Look at each diagram carefully and complete the pattern in the empty square.

1

2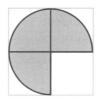

3

4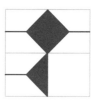

5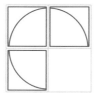

6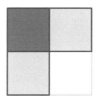

7

8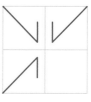

9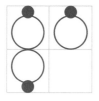

10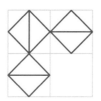

11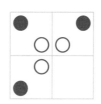

12

13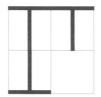

14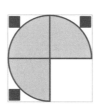

15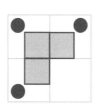

16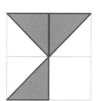

17

18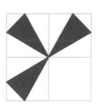

19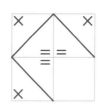

20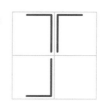

Shapes and values

If you are given the sum of the numbers in each row and the sum of the numbers in each column, then it is easy to find the value of each shape.

In each of these figures, every shape has a different value.

Find the value of each shape or symbol.

1

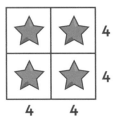

★ = _____

2

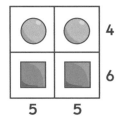

⬤ = _____

⬛ = _____

3

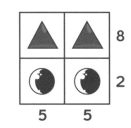

▲ = _____

◐ = _____

4

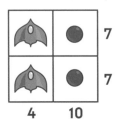

🐦 = _____

● = _____

5

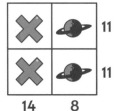

✖ = _____

🪐 = _____

6

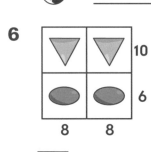

▽ = _____

⬭ = _____

7

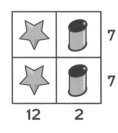

◆ = _____

◐ = _____

8

★ = _____

🛢 = _____

9

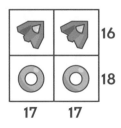

= _____

◎ = _____

Odd one out

In each question **one** of the pictures is different from the other three.

Draw a circle around it.

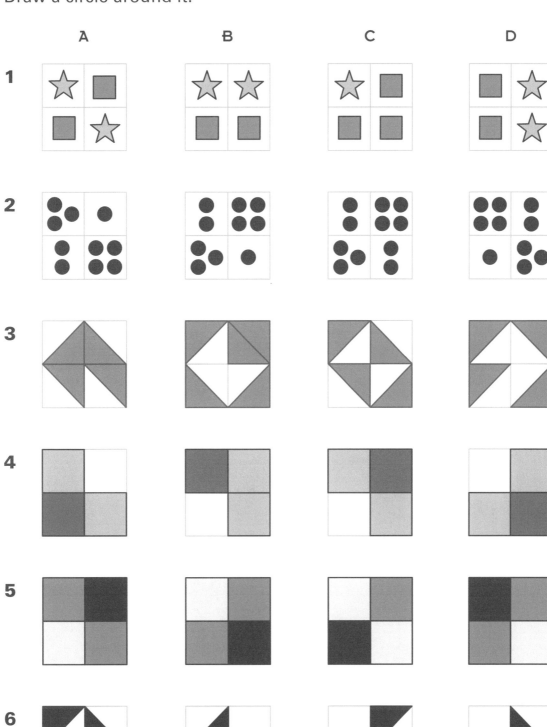

Complete the picture

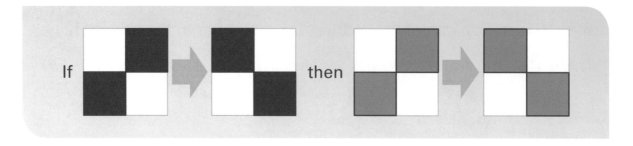

Examine how the first picture changes to become the second picture in each question.

Once you can see a rule, draw the last picture.

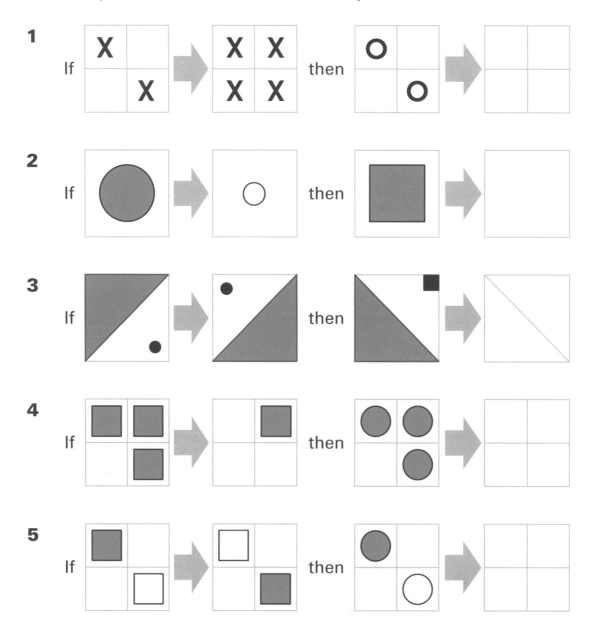

How many squares?

Write down how many small squares are in each shape.

1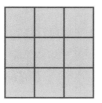

_____

2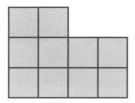

_____

3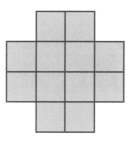

_____

4

_____

5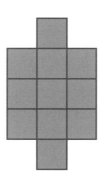

_____

6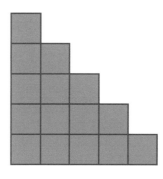

_____

7

_____

8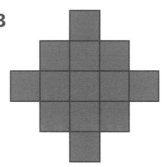

_____

9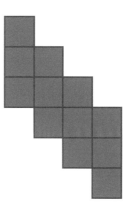

_____

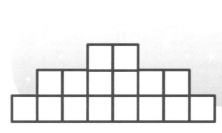

Shading halves

One half of each of these shapes has been shaded.

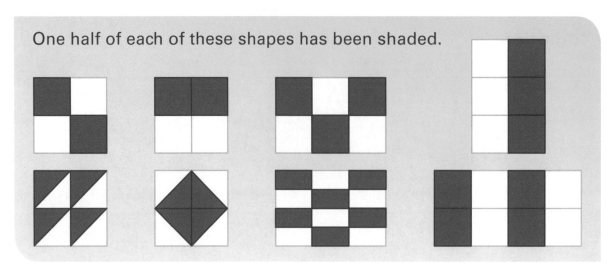

Shade half of each of these squares in as many different ways as you can.

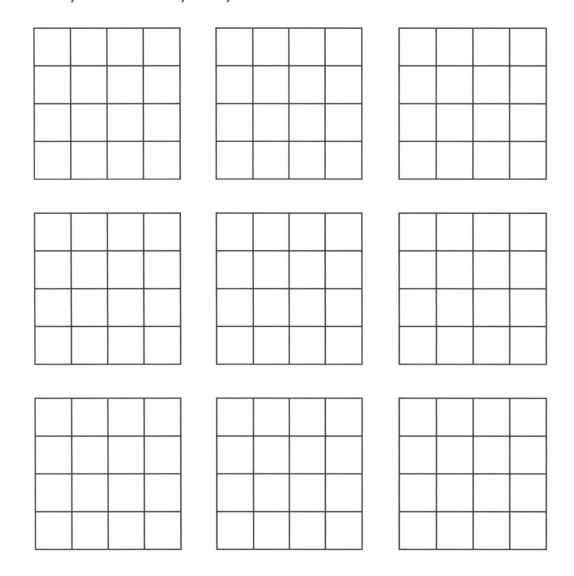

Drawing lines

If we have to draw **one line** to leave two space ships in each part, we can draw:

 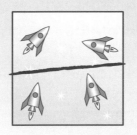 

1 Can you draw **two lines** to leave one space ship in each part?

2 Can you draw **two lines** to leave one space ship in each part?

3 Draw **three lines** to leave one space ship in each part.

a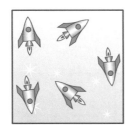

b

working Mathematically

No threes

 Equipment: small counters

Try to add three more crosses in each grid without making a line of three crosses in any column, row or diagonal.

Try two different ways for each. Experiment using counters.

1

	X	
		X

	X	
		X

2

	X	
	X	

	X	
	X	

3

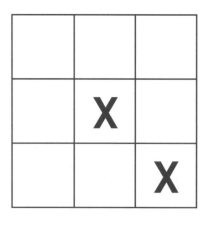

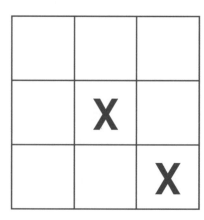

Balancing act

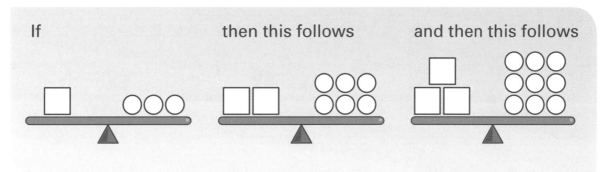

| If | then this follows | and then this follows |

Given the first balance, draw what follows on the other balance.

1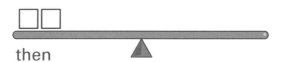

2

3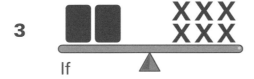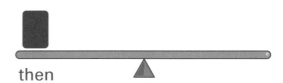

4

5

6

Balance

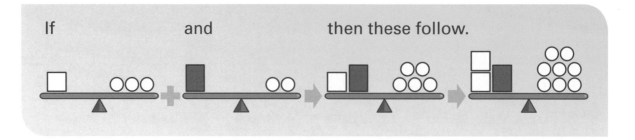

If   and   then these follow.

In each question two balances are given. Work out what should be on the right-hand side of the third balance.

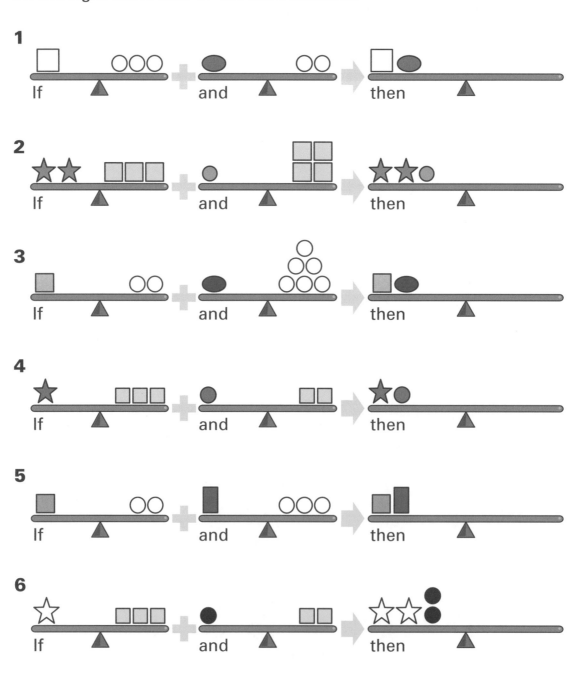

Working Mathematically

Find your balance

In each question two balances are given. This time each shape has a value.

Work out the value of the third balance.

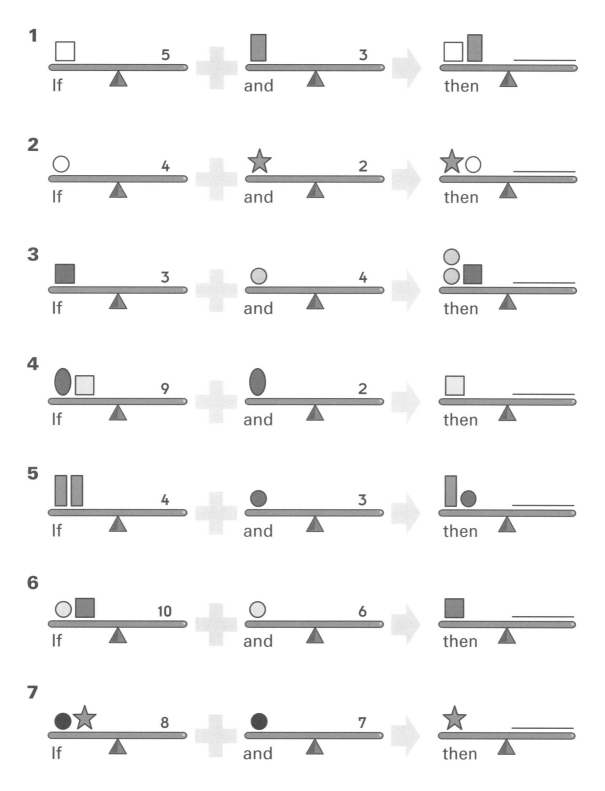

1 If ☐ 5 and ▮ 3 → then ☐▮ _____

2 If ○ 4 and ★ 2 → then ★○ _____

3 If ▪ 3 and ● 4 → then ●●▪ _____

4 If ⬭☐ 9 and ⬭ 2 → then ☐ _____

5 If ▮▮ 4 and ● 3 → then ▮● _____

6 If ○▪ 10 and ○ 6 → then ▪ _____

7 If ●★ 8 and ● 7 → then ★ _____

Number of pins?

1   The smallest number of pins that I need to attach one square piece of paper to a noticeboard is four.

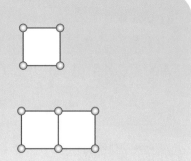

The smallest number of pins that I need to attach two square pieces of paper is six.

a   How many pins for three pieces of paper? _____

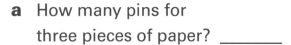

b   How many pins for four pieces of paper? _____

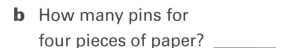

2   The number of pins that I need to attach one triangular piece of paper to a noticeboard is three, two triangular pieces of paper is five.

a   How many pins for three pieces of paper? _____

b   How many pins for four pieces of paper? _____

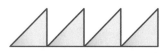

3   This time I need three pins to attach one triangular piece of paper to a noticeboard and four pins to attach two triangular pieces of paper.

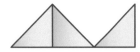

a   How many pins for three triangular pieces of paper? _____

b   How many pins for four triangular pieces of paper? _____

Grid puzzles

Study the first three square puzzles that have been done for you.
Then try to complete the other square puzzles.

Gridlock

Find the shape patterns, and then complete each grid by drawing in the correct shape.

1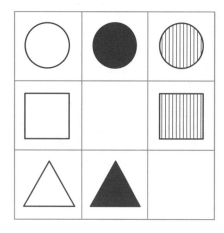

2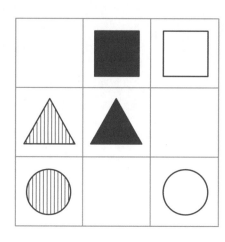

3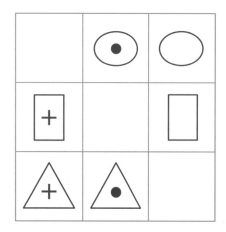

4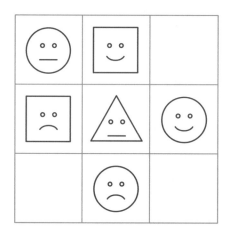

5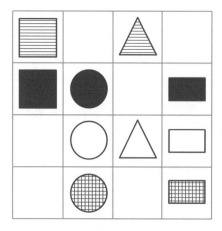

6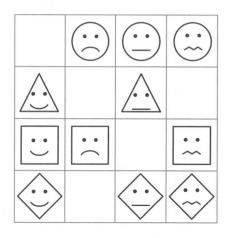

Working Mathematically